Anger

Also by Andrew D. Lester
from Westminster John Knox Press

The Angry Christian: A Theology for Care and Counseling
Hope in Pastoral Care and Counseling
It Takes Two: The Joy of Intimate Marriage (coauthor with
    Judith L. Lester)
Pastoral Care with Children in Crisis
*When Children Suffer: A Sourcebook for Ministry with Children
    in Crisis*

Anger
Discovering Your Spiritual Ally

Andrew D. Lester

Westminster John Knox Press
LOUISVILLE • LONDON

Scripture quotations, unless otherwise indicated, are from the New Revised Standard Version of the Bible, copyright © 1989 by the Division of Christian Education of the National Council of the Churches of Christ in the U.S.A., and are used by permission.

Scripture quotations marked JB are from *The Jerusalem Bible,* copyright © 1966, 1967, 1968 by Darton, Longman & Todd, Ltd., and Doubleday & Co., Inc. Used by permission of the publishers.

Scripture quotations marked NEB are taken from *The New English Bible,* © The Delegates of the Oxford University Press and The Syndics of the Cambridge University Press, 1961, 1970. Used by permission.

Book design by Drew Stevens
Cover design by Crawford Williams Creative
Cover art: © *Getty Images/Farinaz Taghavi*

First edition
Published by Westminster John Knox Press
Louisville, Kentucky

This book is printed on acid-free paper that meets the American National Standards Institute Z39.48 standard. ∞

PRINTED IN THE UNITED STATES OF AMERICA

07 08 09 10 11 12 13 14 15 16 — 10 9 8 7 6 5 4 3 2 1

Library of Congress Cataloging-in-Publication Data

Lester, Andrew D.
　　Anger: discovering your spiritual ally / Andrew D. Lester. — 1st ed.
　　　　p. cm.
　　　"This book is based on research published in more detail in The angry Christian : a theology of care and counseling published in 2003 by Westminster John Knox Press"— Acknowledgments.
　　　Includes bibliographical references.
　　　ISBN-13: 978-0-664-22499-8 (alk. paper)
　　　ISBN-10: 0-664-22499-7
　　　1. Anger—Religious aspects—Christianity. I. Title.

　BV4627.A5L45 2007
　261.5'15—dc22

2006052991

Contents

Acknowledgments

This book is based on research published in more detail in *The Angry Christian: A Theology of Care and Counseling*, published in 2003 by Westminster John Knox Press. That book developed out of a research project made possible by a grant from the Henry Luce III Fellows in Theology program. This excellent program of scholarship opportunities for theologians is offered and administered by the Association of Theological Schools in the United States and Canada and funded by The Henry Luce Foundation, Inc. My appreciation is expressed to Mr. Henry Luce, III, then Chairman and CEO of the Foundation (now deceased), John W. Cook, then President (now retired), and Michael F. Gilligan, then Program Director for Theology and now President and CEO, who have been so instrumental in the success of this program.

This Luce Fellowship program is administered through the Association of Theological Schools in the United States and Canada. My deep gratitude is expressed to Dan Aleshire, Executive Director, and to Matt Zyniewicz, then Coordinator of Faculty Grant Programs, for their investment of time and energy in this program.

I am grateful to Westminster John Knox Press for granting permission to use material from both of these previous books on anger, sometimes verbatim, and also material from *It Takes Two: The Joy of Intimate Marriage*, coauthored by my wife, Judy, and me in 1998.

Most of this project was finished during a sabbatical granted for the academic year 2000–2001 and a Summer Research Grant awarded for the summer of 2001. I am thankful for the support of the trustees, administration, and faculty of Brite

Divinity School of Texas Christian University, who were responsible for these awards.

Amy Cooper and Carol Younger, both accomplished writers, friends, and fellow church members, have critiqued this manuscript and enabled me to shape it into a much more readable form.

Stephanie Egnotovich, Executive Editor at Westminster John Knox Press, has worked with me on at least four books. Once again she offered steadfast affirmation and support, always going the second mile with her consultation. Her insight about style and content are greatly appreciated, and her suggestions make the book much more reader friendly!

I am grateful to those persons—students, counselees, seminar participants, and friends—who have allowed me to share their struggles with anger. Some of them have graciously permitted me to include part of their experience in these pages. Although names and some data are changed, everything else in the illustration reflects their actual stories.

The dedication pages to *Coping with Your Anger: A Christian Guide* and *The Angry Christian: A Theology for Care and Counseling*, include the following:

> To Wayne E. Oates
> who first taught me how
> to deal creatively with anger

As I noted in the acknowledgments in *The Angry Christian*, Wayne was my professor, advisor, friend, pastor, and colleague. His gifts to my family and me are too numerous to recount, but one of them was his witness to effective ways of thinking theologically and ethically about anger. From him I learned to express more creatively this aspect of my being. He died in 1999. I remain grateful for his gracious blessings.

Judy, my wife and partner of forty-six years, read and critiqued this material from her perspective as a marriage and family therapist, offering ideas that resulted from her use of this material in her therapeutic work. I am exceedingly grateful for all she gives to our relationship, particularly her patience when I become preoccupied during the last months of the publishing process.

Preface

I have been interested in anger for many years and wrote my first book on the subject, *Coping with Your Anger: A Christian Guide*, in 1983. This book proposed what I call the "threat model" for understanding anger. This model suggests that the experience of anger is an alarm system that warns the self of a threatening event either in the environment or in mental images. Since then, and especially in the last decade, there has been significant new scientific research on anger that expands this concept.

First, significant developments in technology have propelled the neurosciences into research of the brain, which was until now impossible. We now know much more about the chemical processes by which the brain interprets events to be threatening and then mobilizes us for flight or fight.

Second, a school of thought referred to as narrative theory has been developing within psychology, psychotherapy, and other social sciences, and it makes a major contribution to our understanding of the self. This perspective on personality explains how each of us constructs our own interpretation of events, a central aspect of the "threat model." We now understand how our values and belief systems shape what we perceive to be threatening. These new insights explain why people become angry at different life circumstances.

Both of these developments informed my second book on the subject, *The Angry Christian: A Theology for Care and Counseling*. Furthermore, I used biblical material and theological concepts to develop a more thorough Christian understanding of anger and demonstrated how a revised theology of anger can inform our ethics. I also show how anger, though usually seen as a spiritual enemy, can actually be a spiritual ally, and explore situations in which anger is in fact the most loving response.

With all this new research, it became clear that *Coping with Your Anger* needed to be updated for the general public. The new research material was so extensive, however, that it became clear a completely new book was needed. Thus this book, *Anger: Discovering Your Spiritual Ally*, takes the place of *Coping with Your Anger*. The threat model continues to be a central theme, but the material is now informed by the recent scientific, social science, and theological developments that are included in the more elaborate *The Angry Christian: A Theology for Care and Counseling*.

My perspectives are limited by my particular experience of life. I am a late, late middle age, Anglo American, heterosexual male, speaking from within the Protestant tradition. I am the oldest of six children, having lived my first ten years in a rural area and the rest of my life in urban areas. These aspects of my identity have shaped my life in ways that are probably different from yours. I trust that you will translate my ideas into your own narrative as informed by your age, gender, sexual orientation, ethnic and cultural background, and faith tradition—not to mention the uniqueness of your family of origin and traumatic experiences that you have endured.

1

Reconsidering Anger

Why are you reading a book on anger? Probably for the same reasons I am writing it. Both you and I have experienced the destructive path that anger cuts through lives—including our own. Each of us can give personal examples of times when anger has caused family conflict and broken relationships. We have seen mishandled anger create alienation in marriages, in partnerships, and within extended families. We have seen and experienced "head-on collisions" between angry people who hold different social, cultural, and political ideas and values. We want to get along with other people and avoid conflict so that we and our children can live in peace. We long for the day when the "lion can lie down with the lamb," as Isaiah 11:6 is so often paraphrased.

If you are reading this book, you are probably a Christian, and you are probably angry, or concerned that someone is angry with you. You're probably uncomfortable with that anger and not feeling good about how you are expressing it or reacting to it. You may also be disturbed because anger and conflict are occurring within a relationship that is very important to you—with a spouse, a parent, a roommate, a child, a best friend, or a coworker. Perhaps you are worried about the bad effect this anger is having on this relationship, or frightened by what you fear will happen if things don't change. So you have picked up this book, hoping it will offer some ideas to help you make sense of your anger, and offer some guidance in handling this anger and conflict more creatively.

This book is written for these same reasons. I have sat with many people over the years whose lives were bogged down by anger. I have watched parents alienate children, spouses come unglued, colleagues sabotage each other, and churches split. So much of it seemed unnecessary. If only people understood where anger comes from, both their anger and the anger that they experience from others would be more easily understood and creatively handled. They could learn how to take responsibility for why they are angry, communicate more openly about differences, and express their anger more creatively.

I invite you to explore in the following chapters some of what is bothering you about anger, and some of the basic feelings and ideas about the subject that you bring with you to this book. Each chapter takes on a particular issue that many Christians raise about this powerful emotion.

The rest of this chapter briefly discusses three underlying issues: (1) the three directions of our anger: toward other people, toward ourselves, and toward God, (2) the influence of our past experiences with anger, and (3) what some people learn from their Christian faith.

ANGER AT OTHERS

Romantic notions of love with which we're all familiar suggest that love and anger are unrelated. But that is simply not true—love cannot escape anger! When two persons with different personalities and different histories bring a variety of life experiences, values, and worldviews into a close relationship, there is bound to be conflict. This includes relationships between parents and children. Before their first birthday, children have ideas about what they want and need, and those ideas begin to create conflict. The potential for anger between children and parents is there from then on.

My wife, Judy, and I have often said at marriage enrichment retreats, and in our book,[1] that figuring out what to do with anger was the most difficult adjustment we had to make when we got married. We did not handle conflict creatively, and when we were angry, we usually retreated into silence and withdrawal. Not surprisingly, this caused tension between us and led to feelings of emotional distance. Our unresolved conflict interfered with our intimacy and our growth as a couple. Marital conflict, whether "cold" or "hot," interrupts intimacy for long periods during which a marriage can be worn down and torn apart in ways that are difficult to repair.

We made the mistake of thinking that because we loved each other we should never get angry. But eventually, our need to learn new ways of thinking about anger motivated my first journeys into the literature on this subject. The insights I gained led to creative new ways of dealing with anger. Happily, these insights also led to more intimacy in our marriage.[2]

You may be in the midst of major conflict with important people in your life and looking for ways to handle it creatively. You may struggle with how to handle your own anger toward your spouse, children, parents, neighbors, colleagues, or fellow church members. Perhaps you express your anger with volatile words and actions, and you are plagued by shame and guilt over your behavior. Much to your embarrassment, you know that your anger has wounded others. And now you are seeking ways to deal with your anger that do not hurt others, ways that stay within the boundaries of love.

You may, of course, find yourself interested in this book because of significant levels of ongoing anger you feel toward persons, institutions, corporations, denominations, or government at any level. You may be angered by their attitudes, decisions, incompetence, or insensitivity. We are confronted every day with the anger in our culture over issues such as the war in Iraq, stem cell research, global warming, and the desire of gays and lesbians to marry, join churches, adopt children, and become ordained. We see these conflicts ripping the fabric of our society. Nearly all of us have experienced the conflict and bitterness that splits congregations, divides denominations, and causes estrangement within and between institutions about problems that we consider moral issues. Your beliefs put you on one side or the other of these cultural conflicts, and you wonder as a Christian what to do with your anger at the ideas of those on the other side. I will discuss the whole issue of anger and justice in chapter 4.

Anger can create alienation and chaos in marriages, partnerships, extended families, parent/child relationships, and friendships—making them painful and shortening their life span. But anger *doesn't have to be destructive*. The capacity for anger is part of our creation in the image of God—something purposefully granted to us by the Creator that has positive purposes (see chaps. 2, 3, and 4). This issue is so important that I frequently mention it in this book. I discuss the connection between anger and love in chapter 4, and show how anger can be a path into a deeper intimacy in chapter 7.

You wouldn't have picked up this book if you didn't want to learn something about handling anger more creatively. So in chapter 5 I present a process for handling anger in life-enhancing ways rather than in life-destroying ways. I tell you how to recognize and acknowledge your anger, how to calm your body down so that reason and will can direct your response, how to uncover the threats that make you angry in the first place, how to evaluate the validity of these threats, and how to express your anger in creative, rather than destructive, ways—building community and relationships, rather than harming them.

ANGER AT YOURSELF

You may be frustrated, despondent, or angry with yourself for mistakes, weaknesses, and other failures both real and imagined. Most people have high expectations for themselves, and when we fall short, it is easy to feel threatened by our own actions and then angry with ourselves. We may accept the guilt and shame, or we may hide from our accountability by blaming others. In either case, we know down deep that we are angry with ourselves.

What does our faith offer to deal with this anger so it does not leak out on other people, particularly those we love? In reading this book, you'll learn how to understand anger at yourself, how to change self-defeating patterns of behavior, and how to find effective ways to accept God's grace and mercy.

ANGER AT GOD

Like many Christians, you may either consciously or unconsciously be angry with God. Why? You may feel deep inside that God has let you down by not protecting you or someone you love. An accident, death, disease, divorce, a problem with a child, or any other difficulty may have made you wonder how a good and loving God, a God who you thought was in control of the world—who holds the "whole world in his hands"—couldn't prevent a tragedy you have endured. The covenant you imagined between God and the followers of Jesus, including yourself, has been broken. Your relationship with God seems strained. Indeed, your anger may have led to a feeling of distance, even alienation from God. And that has led you to questions and doubts that are new for you. And you may have no clue about how to deal with this anger. But there are ways you can learn to handle your anger, and I will show you how, especially in chapter 7.

OVERCOMING ANGER FROM YOUR PAST

The truth is, for most of us, that no one taught or showed us ways to understand anger or effectively deal with angry feelings. It is a rare family that carefully and intentionally provides good "anger management" training for the children. Usually parents, and other caregivers, simply pass on what they have learned by witnessing how anger was handled in *their* families. So you may notice patterns about what makes people angry and how they express it that go back several generations. When people marry, they bring different styles from their families, creating conflict in how they parent and deal with anger. Of course, we are also watching our neighbors, our peers, our coaches, and other significant adults as we pick up various ways to handle anger. Who in your history are you most similar to?

I was carefully taught to "be nice," and it was clear that being nice meant not expressing anger. As a result, I grew up afraid of anger and uncomfortable around conflict. If you grew up this same way, you may have been punished if you expressed any anger, even when it was justified. You couldn't push your sister down, hit your brother, fight, get mad, raise your voice, pout, slam the door, or use bad language.

In many families if a child dares to get angry with a brother or a sister, what does the child hear? "Shame on you!" Or "You shouldn't feel that way about your sister." Or "It's not nice to fight with your brother!" And if a child dares to get angry with a parent, she will hear, "Don't talk that way to me!" and perhaps be punished. Parents find it difficult to focus on "why" a child is angry, because they often believe that the anger itself is unacceptable. So many of us grew up hiding our anger behind plastic smiles, which leads to dishonest communication about emotions.

If you have grown up in circumstances such as those I have described, it is likely that you struggle with your anger because any feeling of anger, much less expression of anger, makes you feel that you have done something bad. Why do some people feel so guilty and ashamed about feeling angry? Most of us were raised to believe that being nice, thoughtful, and accepting of others helps make good friends and contributes to a cordial and smooth-running society, not to mention family. Anger, in contrast, can cause distance, conflict, and even alienation. When we feel that our anger disrupts our social, professional, or family environment, we can feel guilty or ashamed.

I watched a lawyer become so upset in a church business meeting that she verbally attacked a committee chair by accusing him of lying. Her anger was rooted in a long-standing personal feud with this chairperson. She was so embarrassed by her outburst and accusations that she left the church. She told me later that she was simply "too ashamed of myself and my angry outburst to ever appear in that church again."

If she had understood more about the original anger, perhaps she could have dealt with it more creatively, a process we will describe in chapter 5.

Perhaps you can remember times in your childhood when your anger got the better of you and an angry outburst quickly led you to feel ashamed of your behavior. I still have vivid memories of a fight I had with another seventh-grade boy.

When Ira moved into our school he was the only boy in my class smaller than me. For reasons I never understood, he picked on me constantly. His favorite trick was to jump on my back when I wasn't looking. I tried to ignore him, be nice to him, and avoid fighting, but his assaults continued. It became difficult to control, much less hide, my anger. Finally, one day when Ira jumped on my back, my growing anger exploded. I threw him over my head onto the basketball court and began beating his head on the asphalt. When the coach pulled me off, Ira was bleeding and I was shaking with a mixture of rage and fear.

You can imagine, given the emphasis in my family to steer clear of all anger, how ashamed I felt for losing my temper. I never told my parents about it and was truly sorry. Most significantly for my future, I promised I would never get that angry again. I became afraid of my anger. Not until I was an adult did anyone help me understand that my anger was justified in this situation, even if my actions were inappropriate.

Discomfort with being angry may be rooted in an experience or event that left you afraid of your own anger. Many of us do everything we can to avoid being angry—at least openly. We even deny anger that we actually are feeling with words such as

"Oh, it's nothing" or "I'm fine" or by laughing instead of letting the anger show. In any case, your past experiences with anger affect how you think and feel about anger as an adult. Pause for a moment and remember these events. What happened? How did you feel about yourself afterward? What did you decide about anger?

But perhaps you grew up in a home where anger was so freely expressed that it was used constantly to batter other members of the family. Whether verbal or physical, this anger was probably painful for you, even when it was aimed at other members of the family. Much of the time you may not have understood the anger and felt that it was unjustified. Yelling, screaming, beatings, or storming out the door might have been the order of the day. This could have affected you in either of two ways.

One possibility is that you copy what you learned in your family, using loud, aggressive anger to punish others for daring to think differently than you do. To this very day you may use intense anger to win arguments. Whether you are really angry or not, you may use angry words to intimidate your family and others in order to get your way. You may have become over the years a chronically angry person, suffering from what I describe in chapter 6 as the "porcupine syndrome." That is, you feel constantly threatened by other people and events, which makes you use much of your energy to defend yourself or attack others.

Another possible response is that you were wounded by this abusive anger in your background. Past verbal or physical abuse may make it difficult for you to relate to others effectively. You may fear that you are now repeating the pattern with your own children. Perhaps you are looking for ways to effectively deal with your anger at people in your past who wounded you; you want to rid yourself of your anger because it continues to affect you.

Being exposed to someone's anger—whether at home, at work, in the store, on the road—can be a scary and disturbing experience.

Pam Johnson, twenty-eight, and Robert Caldwell, thirty-four, were in the same small counseling group. They shared a similar struggle because Pam's father had been an alcoholic and Robert's mother had been a problem drinker. Both Pam and Robert had experienced destructive outbursts of anger from a drunken parent. Pam's father had been very happy when sober, but when drunk he had often beaten her with his belt or with the long chain of keys he carried to work. Robert had dreaded coming home from school, never knowing when his mother would have had too much to drink. "When she had," Robert said, "the whole house would shake with her yelling and screaming." Both had been frightened by their experience and had sworn they would not be angry as adults. Pam had vowed never to lay a hand on a child, and Robert had vowed never to raise his voice.

Pam and Robert were in this counseling group because they were having difficulty feeling any emotion, particularly anger, and this was interfering with their ability to function as spouses and parents. Their early experiences had taught them to fear anger. To succeed in squelching their anger, however, they tried to cut off all emotion, which made it difficult to relate effectively to their loved ones. They were so uncomfortable with emotion that they often wanted their spouses and children to stifle their emotional responses, as well. A person who doesn't feel anything finds it difficult to live an abundant life, because emotions such as joy, awe, passion, and even grief are the key to the most enriching experiences in life. I discuss throughout the book the problems caused by the inability or unwillingness to identify and learn to creatively express our anger. We will see that everyone feels anger (chap. 2), that the Bible supports both the feeling and the expression of anger in appropriate circumstances (chaps. 3 and 4), and that there are healthy and unhealthy ways to express anger (chaps. 5 and 6). I hope this book will allow you to hear Jesus' words—that he came to "proclaim release to the captives" and to "let the oppressed go free" (Luke 4:18).

A friend recently skipped a business meeting at his church, explaining, "I knew there would be conflict over the personnel committee recommendations and I just didn't have the heart for it." He knew in advance that he would be angry with several people who were taking a position he thought was a huge mistake. He worried that he might not control his responses and might "say something I would regret." He also knew he would "go home tighter than a drum and never get to sleep." He would not have been reluctant to attend the meeting, however, if he had known how to use his anger constructively, which is one of the lessons I hope this book provides.

What about you? When you sense impending conflict do you get anxious and try to avoid it? Or are you more fearful that your anger will express itself too aggressively for the situation and make you feel embarrassed at what you say? If you do get caught in a situation where anger is expressed, do you try to smooth things over to avoid conflict, regardless of the issues, or fight to win? Do you find yourself saying, particularly to children who are fussing or fighting with each other, phrases like, "Now, now, we shouldn't argue"?

WHAT DID YOU LEARN FROM
THE CHRISTIAN FAITH?

Many churches teach that the capacity for anger is part of our existence as humans and that anger has an appropriate place in the Christian life. But you may be among those Christians who have grown up hearing and believing that good Christians don't express anger in words or actions.[3] You may have heard some Scripture passages presented as proof that Christians should avoid anger.[4] When we examine what the Bible says about anger in chapters 3 and 4, you will find a very different perspective. As we will see, *scientific, biblical, and theological perspectives agree that anger is a normal part of our human life.*

This negative perspective about anger in the Christian tradition could make it difficult for you to identify and admit your anger, much less deal with it creatively. Instead, perhaps you deal with it in one of three uncreative ways: deny or suppress the anger; feel so guilty or ashamed that you forget your anger as soon as the incident is over; or blame your anger on someone's behavior rather than take responsibility for it. Throughout the book I will describe healthier ways of dealing with anger.

Or you may accept your anger but believe you can keep others from knowing about it. You use a lot of energy trying to hide your anger, but in fact, the anger that you try not to show is probably creating problems. You may find yourself expressing it either knowingly or unknowingly in such conflict-causing ways as nagging, sarcasm, procrastination, and other behaviors that serve the purpose of making the other person mad, which is a secret type of revenge. These destructive expressions of anger will be the subject of chapter 6.

Many people believe that by counting to ten, thinking positive thoughts, or "praying without ceasing," they can keep themselves from feeling angry. These actions may help them express their anger more creatively, but don't stop them from being angry. It is possible to work so hard at not being angry that you block out the *feeling* of anger. Perhaps you can truthfully say, "I don't get angry." But this really means that you have used mental tricks to keep yourself from being *aware* of your anger. Don't be misled; these mental games may keep you from *recognizing* your anger, but they don't keep you from *being* angry deep inside. Anger is related to threat, as I note in the next chapter, and we can't live without being threatened; so it is impossible to live without anger.

The truth is that *every human being experiences anger!* Yes, even Christians. Why? Because our capacity for anger is a part of our human nature as created by God. We will explore the fact that anger is something that God purposely included in our personhood, rooted in our brains and nervous systems for a good reason—to help us survive. Anger can actually be the most loving response to many situations, as I will show in chapter 4. And, moreover, *anger can actually serve us as a spiritual friend, a spiritual guide, and a spiritual ally!*—and you will see how this works in chapter 7.

When you deny or suppress your anger, you are ignoring the strong biblical warning that hiding anger is dangerous (Eph. 4:26), which I will explore in chapter 3. We will see that Christians have a responsibility to handle anger in a more honest, loving, and creative manner.

We are well aware of the antagonism, alienation, and animosity that characterize many relationships and disrupt our culture. We also know that a major dynamic causing this hostility is unresolved anger. I believe this book will provide you with a new understanding of anger and invite you to commit yourself to a creative, life-enhancing Christian way of discovering that anger can be your spiritual ally. I hope that it will enable you to keep love and anger connected; to transform estrangement into reconciliation, hate into love, and vengeance into forgiveness. I trust when you finish this book, you will feel more confident in your ability to follow the words addressed to the Ephesians: "Be angry, but do not sin" (4:26).

2

Why Do We Get Angry?

Anger is a powerful, and dangerous, emotion. If we are to cope with it more creatively, we must first understand it. Let's start with a story: You come home from work thirsty and head into the kitchen. The first thing you see is a mess on the counter: bread crumbs everywhere, open peanut butter jar, a used knife, a dirty plate, and an open bottle of soda. Quickly you become angry at Stephen, your fourteen-year-old son, the only one at home. How do you know you're angry?

Your body lets you know first: perhaps your fists clench, face flushes, nostrils flair, jaw muscles tense, teeth grind, blood pressure goes up, and you break into a "cold" sweat. The second clue is usually a spontaneous action, or at least the thought of acting in some way, perhaps yelling, slapping a table, shaking a fist, or slamming a door. So in this case you might rush to the stairs and yell, "Stephen, get down here and clean up this mess!" Why these physical changes and actions? Because anger begins in our brain,[1] which warns us that we are in danger and motivates us to defend against the "enemy." Anger is the physical, mental, and emotional readiness to attack whatever threatens our survival.

13

Now we can answer the question, Why do we get angry? *Anger only occurs when we feel threatened.* That's right, we do not feel anger unless our brain interprets something in our situation as a threat. When a threat occurs, the brain sends a warning to the rest of the body: "Be alert, we are under attack!" The body immediately becomes mobilized to escape, defend, or attack.[2] In the example above, your quick movement toward the stairs and your yelled demand was an "attack" on Stephen. Think how you might have described this situation to a friend and added, "I could have throttled that kid!"—verbalizing your aggressive response.

The threat that makes us angry can be a physical threat, something that puts our body's health and well-being in danger.[3] Circumstances might even be life-threatening, which is why we become angry at careless drivers, bacteria, terrorists, cancer, ambulances that come late, and doctors who give an inaccurate diagnosis. But *most of the time our anger is triggered by psychological threats.* By *psychological* threat, I mean something that we interpret as a threat to our values, our beliefs about right and wrong, our expectations about the way good people should act, and so forth.

Why were you mad at Stephen? Because (1) you value having a clean kitchen, part of being a good homemaker, (2) you believe that good, responsible family members clean up after themselves, (3) you value thoughtfulness, and want your children to grow up being considerate of others, and (4) your son knows the family rules about cleaning up, and you expect him to be obedient—another strong value you have as a parent. In one glance at the counter, your brain instantly recognized that your son's actions had violated these four values. Look at several more examples:

— You are feeling really chilly. You realize that your partner has once again lowered the thermostat, even though you have a sinus infection and already have on two layers of clothes. You are instantly incensed. How do you know? You grit your teeth, clench your fists, and storm into the den where she is reading and stingingly accuse her of "not being a very caring partner." Why are you so upset? Because as soon as you saw that the thermostat had been changed, several values were threatened. First, you expect that the person who loves you will be concerned about your comfort and health. Second, you hate being cold and see no reason why the house should not be kept at a comfortable temperature. Turning the thermostat lower has threatened these two values and triggered the anger. If you have already asked that she please keep the house warm, then your value of being listened to is also threatened, and your anger increased.

—Another driver, talking on a cell phone, passes you on a curve and almost runs you off the road. Your quick anger is expressed in words you hope the children didn't hear. Why the rage? First, you believe that people who use cell phones while driving are at best inconsiderate and at worse dangerous. This driver's actions threatened your values about (1) being considerate of other people, (2) paying attention to the road, not the phone, (3) safe driving, and (4) not putting others at risk.

—Looking again at your watch, and realizing that it is not possible to get to the theater on time, you yell angrily up the stairs, "Can't you ever get ready on time?" Why are you so mad? You put a high value on "being on time." You believe that responsible people are on time so they won't disturb others. So when you realized you would be late, these beliefs were immediately threatened and you became angry. Furthermore, your spouse knows you have these strong feelings, and you believe that good spouses consider the needs and feelings of the partner, so this value was also threatened, and your anger was even stronger.

Stop and think about recent experiences of anger in your own life. Does your anger in those situations make sense? The bottom-line answer: *your values were threatened by the actions of others*. You were *threatened* because values and beliefs that are important to you were ignored, contradicted, or flouted. For obvious reasons, I call this the "threat model" for understanding anger.

Where do our values and beliefs come from? All our lives, we have been forming ideas and beliefs about what is good and bad, right and wrong, fair and unfair, Christian and unchristian. They become our values, our philosophy about the "way things ought to be." These values are constructed out of our own unique history and the influences of our family, church, school, gender, ethnic group, generation, and religious tradition.

Think about situations that have made you angry in the last several months. Do you know what triggered your anger? Can you identify the values that were threatened? What ideas do you have about right and wrong, fairness, justice, good and bad, and the "way things ought to be" that were threatened? What belief about how family and friends should relate is being contradicted by someone with whom you are angry? Below are some categories of threats that are typical in day-to-day life and might inform your search for the threats that trigger your anger.

THREATS IN DAILY LIFE

A secure sense of personal identity is basic to mental and spiritual health. We value holding all the pieces of our identity together and feeling "whole." Most of what follows is concerned with threats to aspects of our self: our self-esteem, personal integrity, the special people and relationships that are so important to us, the groups with which we are so identified, and even our possessions. We will also talk about other threats to our extended self, such as our dreams and plans for the future, and our moral values. Events such as a divorce, bankruptcy, rejection, serious health problems, or the death of a loved one *threaten those things we hold dear,* and our response includes anger.

Threats to Self-Esteem

Self-esteem is related to how we feel about ourselves, but also to what we want others to think about us. Most of us want to be liked, respected, popular, trusted, and admired. When something happens that affirms us, such as getting a promotion, earning a pay raise, being elected to an office, or receiving flowers from our spouse or an unexpected kiss from one of our children, our self-esteem soars. But our self-esteem can be threatened by a failure, an embarrassment, criticism, making a mistake, being left out, being ridiculed—anything that causes us to think others have a lowered opinion of us—and in response we can feel anger. For example:

Anna and her husband, Rich, were asked by Rich's nephew to be godparents for his new baby. Anna was pleased because she had long felt marginalized by Rich's family because of ethnic and religious differences, and the invitation was especially meaningful to her. But soon another relative called with the news that the nephew was still going to ask Rich to be the godfather, but would not be asking Anna to be the godmother. Anna was furious with his whole family. She angrily denounced these in-laws for their "insensitivity, prejudice, and religious bias." She was also angry with her husband and warned him that she would consider him disloyal if he agreed to the nephew's request.

As Anna began to understand her anger, she recognized the threat to her self-esteem—"I let them make me feel terrible about myself." The problem stemmed not only from the relationship between Anna and her in-laws, but from Anna's feeling that she was "lost in the shadow of her husband," an outgoing and popular lawyer and politician. As she said, "I wish I could be recognized as a worthwhile person with my own personality." She had been working for many months to accept herself and reduce her dependence on other people's opinions, but this blatant rejection seriously threatened her self-esteem.

The threat model helped Ana understand that her heated response was a defense against this threat to her self-esteem. Can you remember any time when you have been angry because your sense of worth was threatened?

Threats to Our Ideal Self

We are also threatened when we fall short of our "ideal self." Growing up, you probably learned from family, church, and society that "good" people—those who are respected—are honest, loyal, faithful, hardworking, true to their word, and helpful to others. You also learned how good parents should function, how ideal wives and husbands respond to each other, and what good Christians should do and be. These lessons shaped the development of your ideal self, the kind of person you wanted to become so that everyone would like you.

This ideal self is an important motivating force, pushing and pulling us to attain our goals and fulfill our potential. When our behavior falls short of this ideal—we tell a lie, fudge a report, steal an idea, make a poor investment, parent without creativity, or fail in a relationship—our ideal self is threatened. Ironically, in these circumstances the threat comes from *our own actions*. In response to this threat *we get angry with ourselves*, and the result is that we feel guilt or shame.

Sharon, a mother of two boys, four and two years old, came for counseling because, she said,

"I'm depressed all the time" and I "worry whether I'm a good mother or not." She had these feelings because she was often angry at the boys. Sharon was raised to believe that expressing negative emotions was bad. She had admired the calm, cool way in which her mother kept house and entertained. But as the mother of two rambunctious, curious, active boys, Sharon was unable to keep house the way she had imagined. Therefore, when the boys "messed things up," her ideal self as a housekeeper was threatened and she got angry. Her ideal self also demanded that as a "good" mother she would have "good" children. "Good" to Sharon meant quiet, neat, and helpful, as she had been as a child. When her sons were noisy, messy, and uninterested in helping, her ideal of how she should act as a mother was threatened. As the younger boy began walking and causing more messes, her anger increased. She felt she was abusing them by "tongue-lashing" them and "spanking them too hard," which made her feel guilty.

Sharon's self-esteem was threatened because she was unable to live up to her ideal self (1) as a housekeeper, (2) as an effective mother who could raise "good" children, and (3) as a person who always stayed calm. So she was angry not only with her sons, but also with herself for not accomplishing these goals. Though most of the anger was at herself, it was "leaking out" on her sons because they weren't being "good." But expressing her anger by harshly spanking them seemed to her to be yet another failure. So in her mind, this destructive expression of anger became another threat to her self-expectations.

Personal integrity refers to how we feel when our actions square with our moral commitments. When we violate our own moral standards, or fall short of what we expect of ourselves, then our sense of personal integrity is compromised, our self-esteem is wounded, and we will probably feel threatened and angry. When we speak and act (or fail to speak and act) in ways that violate our conscience, we feel threatened by our own actions. Guilt and shame are two of the feelings that we associate with such situations, but they are often accompanied by anger. Unfortunately, we often blame someone else or blame circumstances for our failures in order to escape these uncomfortable feelings.

Threats to Special People and Relationships

We do not exist in isolation. No person is an island. We extend our sense of self into other people, so that they become part of us. We are interdependent social creatures whose identity is interconnected with other individuals, groups, and institutions. Our investment in people and relationships makes us vulnerable to threat. If some event or person threatens our spouse, parents, children, friends, or one of our heroes, then *we* feel threatened. These people have become part of us and we don't want anybody hurting them. Remember the anger you felt when:

— Another child bullied your son on the playground
— The nursing home treated your parent poorly
— A drunk driver caused an accident that injured your spouse
— Your best friend's spouse cheated on her
— A boyfriend took advantage of your daughter

When someone we love has been victimized, or we perceive him or her to be victimized, we are threatened as if it were ourselves who had been hurt.

As social creatures we depend on significant relationships, our network of family and friends, for security and meaning. When one of our basic relationships is in danger, therefore, we experience anger at the threat. Marital infidelity is often such a threat:

> Barbara called late one night in a panic. She had confessed to her husband, Don, that she had been having an affair for six months. The three of us met the next day. The immediate problem was Don's anger, which he expressed in several forms—disillusionment, hurt, and rage. His first angry reaction was toward Barbara and he described how tempted he was to just "throw her out on the street." Later his anger focused on the other man. As Don talked through his emotional responses he could easily imagine physically "beating up this other man" or at least "exposing the affair at the man's workplace so he would have to resign."

Don's anger was not surprising, but to understand his response we need to examine it in terms of the significance of his marriage. Don received much of his meaning in life from his family. He valued marriage and invested a good portion of his identity in being a stable family man—a good husband and father. The actions of his wife and this other man jeopardized this part of his extended self.

At first he perceived Barbara's behavior as the threat, and most of his anger was directed toward her. Then his need to believe that his wife was more committed than her behavior would indicate took over, and his focus changed to the other man. Don supposed that the other man had "taken advantage" of Barbara's "weaknesses," and his anger became focused on this intruder into his marriage. Later Don identified another threat, namely that other people would see him as a man so weak or unattractive that his wife would "have to find someone else to satisfy her." So some of his anger was toward himself.

Any experience of anger can be a response to multiple threats. Don's experience is an example of the many layers of threat that can exist in one situation. Coping with anger creatively means asking the questions, Why am I threatened? How does this person's behavior threaten my expectations for how they will relate to me? If we don't know all the threats, we can't respond as creatively as we would like.

Threats to Special Groups and Institutions

We are also invested in groups, such as social clubs, businesses, churches, and sports teams. These broader relationships also contribute to our identity. These groups can become a broader family in which we deeply invest ourselves. We don't like it when they are attacked, or ridiculed, or suffer failures.

Think of rabid sports fans, fiercely loyal to their teams. Fans hang team pictures on their walls, wear shirts and hats with team symbols, and collect autographs from the players. They strongly identify with these teams, particularly with their success. We see angry fans in the stands yelling at coaches, players, and particularly at "blind" umpires and "incompetent" referees. Anything that gets in the way of their team winning, such as opposing teams, critical sports writers, and coaches with losing records, create a serious threat.

What is the threat? Some fans become so identified with their team that personal identity becomes inseparable from the team. The value they place in competition and success, the belief in victory, the need to be heroic—all are threatened by losing. Those who cause the loss are threats, and they trigger intense anger. Many other cultural factors are involved, but overidentification between fan and team is the major issue.

Angry behavior by parents attending sports events in which their children are involved is a cultural concern. Many project their own needs to win onto the children, and then become threatened by their children's mistakes, the choices of the coaches, and, of course, the referees. The parents' expression of anger often becomes a source of embarrassment to the children. Sometimes the anger erupts in physical, even fatal, attacks on officials and other parents. Many youth leagues have had to give parents warnings or expel them. What model is this for the children?

Threats to Our "Things"

Have you ever become angry with movers who scratched favorite pieces of furniture, or a child who spilled grape juice on a good rug, or the person who scratched the side of your car in a parking lot, or the devastation caused by a broken water heater? Christians have traditionally been warned against investing in possessions. Being "materialistic" is frowned upon. But in real life we become attached to and value possessions such as homes, cars, heirlooms, art objects, and family pictures. We invest these material things with meaning. Certain belongings symbolize a significant event or relationship and are important to us. If they are harmed, scratched, broken, or stolen we are threatened and get angry.

Linda came home one evening to find her house ransacked and burglarized. She was threatened by this invasion of boundaries. She became fearful and angry with those who had, as she said, "treated her possessions so disrespectfully" and caused her to have an ongoing sense of vulnerability. She felt the most anger about the theft of jewelry given to her by her mother and husband, both now deceased. The jewelry had served as an ongoing connection with these two important people in her life.

Once we are aware of these attachments, investments, and symbolic meanings we give to our possessions we can better understand a child who gets angry when one of her favorite toys breaks; the teenager who becomes livid when someone puts a dent in his car; and the neighbor who is angry that a baseball has once again been thrown into her flower garden.

Threats to Future Hopes and Dreams

God has given us the capacity to anticipate and plan the future. We have been created with the ability to project our imagination into the future and create "future stories" that include our hopes and dreams.[4] Your hopes and dreams have become part of you, and if a person or event threatens your future, you will feel threatened and angry. Part of what is happening when a person is angry at a partner for leaving, an employer for being fired, or a child for flunking out of college is that dreams for the future are now threatened by serious changes in our life situation. Take a health crisis for example:

> While caring for her dying mother, Janet began to imagine becoming an ordained minister. The dream developed into a sense of call as she made plans to attend seminary. As she was beginning her studies she became ill and was diagnosed with a neurological disease. In the last four years she has suffered through several major attacks, the most recent leaving her paralyzed except for her right arm and her head. She

made an amazing recovery from this attack and during her rehabilitation learned to use what mobility she did have to take care of herself and live independently. During this ordeal she never lost sight of her goal of being a minister.

In our last visit, however, Janet was visibly upset and angry. Her physical therapist had told her that further work in the rehabilitation unit would not be helpful. Janet was aware that she had not been making progress recently, but tried to ignore this disturbing fact. To hear the expert say that no more could be done was quite a shock. As we talked, Janet expressed her anger at what she calls her "disease process" because it threatened her future story of entering ministry.

Why was Janet so angry? Her future story was threatened by dreaded possibilities. She had continued hoping that she would learn to walk again, assuming she would need to walk to be an effective minister. Now her dream was shattered and she was threatened, anxious, and angry. Her anger was expressed toward the therapist, but she was also mad at her disease and at God for not bringing healing.

The future can also represent a threat. Dreams about threatening events from the past can wake us up at night, or we may lie awake at night anticipating an event in the future that makes us angry: what if she divorces me, what if he is deployed again to Iraq, what if the chemotherapy doesn't work, what if the accident causes a miscarriage, and so forth. When we imagine these possibilities coming true, the hopes and dreams in which we are invested are threatened—leading, of course, to anger at those who cause the threatening circumstances.

Threats to Moral Values

Our values and beliefs include very specific ideas about morality: what is right and wrong. Current debates over abortion, homosexuality, and stem-cell research, for example, spark anger on both sides. The ideas of those on the other side are a threat to our own moral values and belief system. The anger stirred up by these controversies demonstrates how threatened people feel when their strongly held belief systems are under attack.

The diverse moral beliefs that currently divide our country, shape political allegiances, and cause major conflict in local churches and denominations are deeply rooted in our value systems. We have become identified with them—they are "ours," therefore, *we* become seriously threatened and intensely angry when these morals are disregarded, ridiculed, disagreed with, or made legal or illegal by the other side. The degree of threat can be intense, and the anger strong.

Next time you are angered by something in the media, ask yourself, "Which of my values has been threatened?" In chapter 4 I will explore how we as Christians can assess the threats and describe some appropriate responses.

CONFLICT IN RELATIONSHIPS

You may be reading this book because conflict has raised the intensity of your anger. This conflict may be focused on a larger system such as the justice system, or on an institution such as your church, a hospital, or a business. Or your conflict may be with an individual outside the family, such as a boss, neighbor, church member, or doctor. But conflict with those we love and are committed to, such as spouses,[5] partners, parents, children, and dear friends, are probably the biggest challenge. Being angry feels like a threat to the relationship.

We get angry at each other because we all have different ideas about the "way things ought to be." Conflict occurs because of this clash of different values, beliefs, expectations, and ideas of right and wrong, good and bad, and so on, in which each person is highly invested. Each person is threatened by the other person's values, and the conflict results from the defense of our own position.

Suppose one partner believes that tabletops and kitchen counters are for stacking "stuff" just brought home from the office or school, but the other partner thinks that tabletops and counters should always be clean and that "stuff" should be put where it belongs, out of sight in closets and drawers in the appropriate room. Conflict will constantly occur over these different understandings of the "right way to do things" until these partners take time to find a compromise about using tabletops and counter space that both can live with.

Because we are all unique, we do not interpret situations in the same way. Conflict also occurs because something that feels like a big threat to one person presents little threat to another. So one person is highly threatened and feels intense anger while the other feels little threat and therefore only mild irritation. They may share the same value, but one has much more "self" invested in that value.

> Sam and Marguerite agreed that they would limit the amount of sugar their toddler consumed. They and their pediatrician thought that some of his hyper behavior might be related to sugar intake. Sam's mother, however, who often took care of the toddler, felt free to override Marguerite's instructions and wishes. She felt that the restrictions were ridiculous, and that the toddler deserved some "treats" as special attention from his grandmother. So Marguerite was very angry with Sam's mother because two important values were threatened: (1) the belief that sugar was bad for the toddler, and (2) the belief that Sam's mother should respect their decisions as parents. Sam, however, was more understanding of his mother's need to be a doting, "spoiling" grandmother. So much so that he softened his position and asked Marguerite to "back off." He was only mildly angry with his mother and found it hard to realize the intensity of Marguerite's anger.
>
> Marguerite then became irritated at Sam for being "soft" and even "flip-flopping" about their agreement in the face of his mother's dissatisfaction. She was also hurt that Sam seemed to side more with his mother than with her, which threatened her belief that the marriage relationship is primary over family of origin. So, of course, she was angry about what she called his "disloyalty," and her anger grew.

This is another example of the multiple levels of threats that can be present in any given situation. When angry we are wise to ask, "What are all the possible threats that I am feeling in this situation?" To keep digging for other threats will help us understand the anger more completely and, therefore, be more likely to cope creatively with all the threats.

We are often surprised at what makes other people angry: "She just got mad for no reason," or "What in the world got into him?" It doesn't always make sense to us that someone else is upset, frustrated, or irritated. Each person's values and beliefs can be unique, so we do not interpret situations in the same way. We can remind ourselves that they must be threatened or they wouldn't be angry. To understand another person's anger calls for us to put ourselves in their shoes. By listening to what the other person is upset about, we might be able to piece together an answer. Instead of dismissing the anger as unnecessary or immature, we can ask ourselves what that person was threatened by. Understanding how the other person is threatened usually allows us to make a more effective response.

FROM IRRITATION TO RAGE:
THE INTENSITY OF ANGER

Have you ever been frightened by the intensity of your anger? Instead of being simply irritated with a colleague, a spouse, or one of your children, you were surprised at suddenly being enraged. The degree of anger we feel depends on (1) how surprising and devastating the threat feels, and (2) how often the threat has been repeated.

If the threat is minor, such as a child caught up in a TV show who forgets a chore, or a coworker coming late to a meeting, or a friend forgetting a lunch date, or the committee chair being unprepared for the meeting, then you may feel only mildly irritated. If the threat is significant and the possible results disastrous, however, such as the devastating announcement from your spouse that he or she wants a divorce, or the memo that says the business is bankrupt and on Friday you no longer have a job, then our anger may be much more intense.

The intensity of our response depends on the amount of personal investment we have in the values, beliefs, and meanings that are being threatened. If you have been thinking about divorce yourself, you may feel more relief than anger when your spouse brings up the subject. You may be so invested in one side of a church debate that when your ideas are defeated, the threat to your ideals is so strong and your anger so intense that you leave that congregation. The amount of anger you feel in any situation reveals how strongly you hold the particular values and beliefs that have been threatened.

> Heather values special days and believes that if Loren really loved her he would recognize special days such as her birthday, their anniversary, and Valentine's Day. Special days were also very important to her parents. Heather believes that giving gifts on these occasions represents how families show love to each other. When Heather married she expected Loren to behave the same way as she and her family did. When Loren forgets a special day (again!), she feels hurt and angry. Her expectation and need for this affirmation has not been met.
>
> Loren, however, did not come from a family that made much of special days, so he did not anticipate her expectations. He believes that Heather should recognize and value all of the little ways he expresses his love every day. So when she becomes hurt and angry over his lack of response on special days, his belief in showing love each day is threatened and he responds with anger of his own.

What is happening? Why is Heather angry? Her expectation is that a good husband would know about the romantic meanings she attaches to special days and gifts and would respond accordingly. This value is threatened when Loren does not respond, and then she feels unloved. Loren, in contrast, places high value on day-to-day affection and wants Heather to feel his love in his daily actions; he feels threatened because this is "not enough" for Heather.

Remember—when you are angry, it means that something has threatened you. And your God-given response is to be angry. This "threat model" guides us to an important step in coping with anger creatively: *learning to identify when and why we are threatened.* In chapter 5 we will describe a full process of dealing with anger creatively, but one central part of that process is learning to realize that if we are angry, it is not because somebody or something made us angry. Rather it is because somebody or something threatened us, even if the situation was not threatening to others.

So our first responsibility when angry is to understand "why I am angry." Some people find it helpful to follow this thought process: (1) I am angry, therefore I must be threatened. (2) Something has threatened me or something important to me. (3) What is this threat? Answering this third question is crucial to discovering anger as our spiritual ally. This chapter provides plenty of questions that will help you become better at identifying threats. When we recognize particular threats, we can take responsibility for dealing with our anger more creatively and ethically, as we will discuss further in chapter 5.

THE THREAT MODEL AND CHRISTIAN FAITH

You may be wondering how this "threat model" of anger relates to your Christian faith. Does faith contradict these ideas? Does science challenge religion? You will see, both here and in other chapters, that science and our Christian faith are in agreement about what we have learned.

Scientific research, for example, has established that the capacity for anger is deeply imbedded in our brain and neurological system, and anger is activated when something in life threatens us. This capacity for anger is not a recent development, but has been unfolding during our entire biological history, which provides an insight for us based in the first creation story recorded in Genesis 1. When God looked over creation, according to this story, God saw "everything" that had been created, including the female and male creatures, and rejoiced, saying, "it was very good" (1:31). We can assume on the basis of scientific discoveries that the "everything" that God saw and believed to be "very good" included our capacity for anger. In this sense God blessed this emotion. Our capacity for anger, therefore, can be thought of as a gift from God[6] with important purposes: to serve as an alarm signal that warns us when we, and those things we hold dear, are endangered and to prepare us for self-defense—to help us survive.

Most of us assume that God was in some manner the originator of the creation process, therefore responsible for including in humans this capacity for anger. The creation stories in Genesis 1 and 2 make it clear that God intentionally brought our entire physical bodies into existence, including emotionality. Our capacity for anger is an essential aspect of life that was in God's original purpose for creation—helping us to survive and thrive in this world. This capacity is part of what it means to be created in the image of God (*imago Dei*). Christian understandings of anger need to be anchored in our beliefs about creation.

We will see what the Bible says about human anger and about the anger of Jesus and God in the next two chapters.

3

What Does the Bible Say?

You may assume as I did for a long time that Scripture supports the view that "good" Christians should not *show* anger and that the "best" Christians don't even *feel* angry. Years ago, however, one of my mentors in a clinical training residency questioned my ideas about anger. "Where did you get the idea that anger is always bad?" he asked. I was surprised at the question, because I assumed that all Christians believed as I did. Finally I answered, "Well, I guess because the Bible says so." Then he asked where I found support for my argument in Scripture. I had to think hard, but I finally mentioned the story of Cain, who was so angry that he killed his brother Abel, and Jesus' saying in the Sermon on the Mount that being angry was like murder. My mentor challenged my interpretation of both stories and suggested I make a more careful and thorough study of Scripture. I took his advice, and to my surprise discovered that the biblical messages about anger are much different than I had assumed.

As it turns out, many Christians overlook much of what Scripture says about anger, and we do this because of prejudices established over the centuries.[1] The Christian tradition often "spoke" as if Scripture always identifies anger as sinful. Those verses or stories that contradict this position were ignored or misinterpreted. Anger became one of the seven deadly sins. I came to realize that there was another side to the story. As we examine various biblical messages about anger, I invite you to carefully review the data. You may be surprised to learn that Scripture supports many of the conclusions about anger reached by psychologists and neuroscientists.

ANGER CAN LEAD TO SIN, BUT NOT NECESSARILY

We have a choice, when angry, to use it creatively or to allow it to lead us into sin. One of the most basic scriptural truths about anger is that it is not automatically connected with sin.

Cain's Anger

The story about Cain and Abel, which is one of the best-known stories in the Bible, is about sibling jealousy. Cain's experience is instructive. Perhaps, like me, you made the assumption that anger led Cain to kill his brother, and then you jump to the conclusion that to be angry is to sin. But read the story again.

> And the Lord had regard for Abel and his offering, but for Cain and his offering he had no regard. So Cain was very angry, and his countenance fell. The Lord said to Cain, "Why are you angry, and why has your countenance fallen? If you do well, will you not be accepted? And if you do not do well, sin is lurking at the door; its desire is for you, but you must master it."
>
> (Gen. 4:4–7)

As this story passed from generation to generation, and finally into written form, God's reason for not accepting Cain's offering was lost. Perhaps the Lord's words, "If you do well, will you not be accepted?" indicate that Cain had not followed instructions or had not been faithful to some ritual. If so, Cain's anger may have been his response to the threat he felt from guilt or shame. Maybe Cain's anger was related to his loss of self-esteem. Maybe he felt rejected. In any case, Cain was threatened by the event and became "very angry."

Notice that even though Cain "was very angry," he was not accused of sinning. Did the Lord say, "You have no right to be angry" or "Your anger at me is a sin"? No. The issue was not that Cain had become angry, but that being angry made Cain more vulnerable to temptation. To make that point God warned him that "sin is lurking at the door; its desire is for you." All of us have been there; we know that when we are angry we are much more likely to act in ways that are destructive. So God's warning makes good sense. We know that anger is dangerous, but that is different from being sinful.

Anger can work in the service of evil, but it doesn't have to. This story is one of the earliest in Scripture that describes the human freedom to make choices about behavior. The Lord told Cain that he had the opportunity and the responsibility to "master" the anger and choose a nondestructive way of dealing with it. It is not Cain's experience of anger that creates the sin, but his response. First, he allows himself to be threatened by his failure and God's rejection. Second, he chooses a sinful way to express his anger. Cain had the choice: to sin with his anger (which, in fact, he did), or to learn from this experience of anger and enhance his spiritual growth.

Don't Let the Sun Go Down on Your Anger

A similar truth is found in the New Testament. The fourth chapter of the Letter to the Ephesians exhorts readers to lead a life worthy of their calling as Christians, and to become new selves "created according to the likeness of God in true righteousness and holiness." After this magnificent challenge, the author gives specific guidance on how those in Christ should be different from those who are alienated from God. Included is this significant passage about anger:

Be angry but do not sin; do not let the sun go down on your anger, and do not make room for the devil.

(Eph. 4:26–27)[2]

Everyone knows the phrase "do not let the sun go down on your anger," but many of us forget the first part of this sentence, "Be angry." Is the author telling Christians to get angry? Yes and no. He is not ordering them to be angry, but this admonition does affirm the reality that Christians get angry. These words acknowledge that with their different backgrounds, values, and personalities members of the church (as we know from our own experience!) were bound to find themselves angry at each other. The author is not concerned that we experience anger, but about what we do with our anger. Evidently, some were trying not to be angry, ignoring or suppressing it, and ended up sinning with their anger—maybe in ways we will describe in chapter 6.

Throughout the history of Christianity, some Christians have acted as if these verses said, "Don't you dare allow yourselves to get angry; that would be sinful!" As you can see, however, these words make no judgment on the fact that Christians experience anger. The point is the same as God's warning to Cain: we are more vulnerable to sin when we are angry. The author admonishes Christians not to sin when they are angry. In fact, the New English Bible translates it "do not let anger lead you into sin."

How can we sin with our anger? The wise author of Ephesians knows that trying to ignore anger, or pretending we don't have any, or harboring it in our hearts (as warned against in Prov. 14:29 and Matt. 5:21) can lead to destructive behavior. In fact, just a few verses later (v. 31) the author names some of the destructive offspring of unresolved anger: "bitterness," "slander," and "malice." So the readers are warned to take care of their anger promptly, today, before the sun goes down.

Allowing anger to go unattended or unresolved is risky. When we avoid our anger by ignoring it, we are behaving dangerously because ignoring anger's potential harmfulness puts people we care about at risk. Ephesians considers it imperative to deal with anger promptly and "make no room for the devil," thus avoiding any collusion with anger's "dark" side. Notice how closely this parallels God's admonition to Cain, "Sin is lurking at the door, its desire is for you, but you can master it."

BEING "SLOW TO ANGER"

Scripture suggests another way to avoid sinning with our anger: apply the brakes, think it through, ponder the situation. In numerous passages we are told to be "slow to anger."

The Wisdom Sayings

The ancient Hebrews expressed their ideas about human nature in the "Wisdom sayings," some of which are recorded in Proverbs and Ecclesiastes. Christians sometimes misinterpret the passages on anger, assuming that they say a wise person doesn't get angry. Not so. The wisdom sayings are explicitly concerned about those who handle anger poorly. Examine for yourself the following passages.

> One who is quick-tempered acts foolishly . . .
> (Prov. 14:17)

> Whoever is slow to anger has great understanding, but one who has a hasty temper exalts folly.
> (Prov. 14:29)

> One who is slow to anger is better than the mighty, and one whose temper is controlled than one who captures a city.
> (Prov. 16:32)

> Those with good sense are slow to anger, and it is their glory to overlook an offense.
> (Pro

Do not be quick to anger, for anger lodges in the bosom of fools.

(Eccl. 7:9)

Do these Wisdom sayings paint a picture of good humans as those who *never* feel or experience any anger? No. Wise people are those who are *slow* to anger. The advice is about the destructive possibilities that exist when people are quick-tempered, but there is no word here that forbids God's people to experience anger. Instead these wisdom sayings challenge us to take responsibility for evaluating *what* to get angry at, *when* to get angry, and *how* to express the anger.

These verses do *not* suggest that we deny or suppress our anger, but speak instead against temper tantrums, explosive hostility, and other immature and unethical expressions of anger. Anger that is separated from our capacity to think clearly and make careful assessments is perceived as immature. We must be careful with our anger, because anger that boils over usually becomes problem-causing rather than problem-solving.

Qualification for Bishops

The Letter to Titus discusses the characteristics Christians should look for when choosing elders and bishops. A bishop, says the author,

> must not be arrogant or quick-tempered or addicted to wine or violent or greedy for gain; but he must be . . . self-controlled.

(1:7–8)

As with the Wisdom literature, this describes a person who is "self-controlled" rather than "quick-tempered"—certainly not a person who is never angry at all. People who are out of control can become "violent," so these qualifications are found in a mature person who is not easily threatened. Other descriptive words such as "a lover of goodness" and "prudent" (v. 8)

suggest that a person qualified for leadership in the churc
insightful about how to recognize a valid threat, when to ⌐⌐
threatened, what to be angry about, and how to behave when
angry (v. 8). The church does not need leaders who suppress
their anger and allow it to leak out in life-destroying ways.

Producing God's Righteousness?

You may also have heard a verse from James used to argue that
anger of any sort is inappropriate because it sabotages God's
work in the world. But such an interpretation misses the context. Take a look.

> You must understand this, my beloved: let everyone be
> quick to listen, slow to speak, slow to anger; for your anger
> does not produce God's righteousness.
>
> (James 1:19–20)

As you can see, James's admonition is to be "slow" to anger,
rather than to never be angry. Like the passages in Proverbs, the
James passages are concerned with *why* we get angry and *how*
we express it. Furthermore, we must remember that James is
guiding his readers to endure the testing of their faith in order
to "be mature and complete" (1:4). They are to ask God for wisdom and to endure "temptation . . . by one's own desire, being
lured and enticed by it" (1:12, 14). When James addresses "your
anger," therefore, he is concerned about anger that results from
our own immaturity and selfish desires, because *that* kind of
anger does not accomplish God's purposes. Clearly, from
James's perspective, some kinds of anger *do* work toward God's
purposes, and he is not cautioning us against that anger.

None of these biblical texts support the idea that all experiences of anger are sinful. Rather, they point out the importance
of not allowing our own selfishness, immaturity, idolatry, or
spiritual blindness cause us to become threatened unnecessarily, resulting in anger that is not in the service of love.

WHEN ANGER "GOES BAD"

We all know from personal experience how easy it is for anger to "go bad," and Scripture is frequently concerned that our capacity for anger not become a motivator of destructive behavior.

The Sermon on the Mount

The biblical passage most often quoted by those who defend the position that "Christians shouldn't get angry" is from the Sermon on the Mount.

> You have heard that it was said to those of ancient times, "You shall not murder"; and "whoever murders shall be liable to judgment." But I say to you that if you are angry with a brother or sister, you will be liable to judgment; and if you insult a brother or sister you will be liable to the council; and if you say, "You fool," you will be liable to the hell of fire.
>
> (Matt. 5:21–22)

When you first read this passage you may think it says that feeling angry in any situation is the same as committing murder. Many Christians respond to this passage as if Jesus had said, "If you have the slightest feeling of anger in your heart, you are a terrible person and will be judged harshly!" Indeed, I can remember sermons and Sunday school classes when I was a youth in which this verse was used to make people think that in God's sight any experience of anger is the same as killing someone.

Closer examination of the original Greek text, however, reveals a more accurate understanding. The verb *orgizesthai*, which is translated "are angry," is a present participle and refers to continuous action. A more exact translation would be "everyone who is continuously angry" or "everyone who stays angry with a brother or sister." Many translators are more exact than the New Revised Standard Version quote given above. Well-known translator Charles Williams translates this phrase, "everyone who harbors malice against his brother," and the New English Bible reads, "anyone who nurses anger against his brother."

So you can see that Jesus is not talking about *every* experience of anger. Rather he *is* concerned about anger that lies unresolved in the heart, festering until it bursts forth in abusive behavior—such as insulting others (v. 22) and calling them fools (v. 22). Reflecting the verse in Ecclesiastes, Jesus points out that anger nursed and fertilized in one's heart becomes destructive of human personality and like murder is judged negatively by God. If we allow anger to simmer demonically inside us ("[lodge] in the bosom of fools"), it will poison our relationships.

Jesus is supporting the idea that when you let "the sun go down on your anger" you give opportunity to the demonic. Perhaps this is why Jesus follows his statement about anger with an admonition to work toward reconciliation of conflicts (vv. 23–25). When our anger is allowed to alienate relationships and destroy individuals, we certainly deserve judgment. But this does not mean that every time we get angry we have sinned. In fact, as we will see later, in some circumstances anger is, believe it or not, the most loving response.

The King James Version has an extra phrase: "whosoever is angry with his brother *without a cause*." You may recall hearing a person excuse some destructive form of anger (such as revenge, jealousy, or a long-standing resentment) because somebody had given that person a reason (a "cause") to be angry. But the oldest manuscripts of the Bible do not include this phrase, and present-day translations of the Bible include it only in the margins. I have often wondered if this phrase was added by a scribe who knew personally that all people get angry and wanted to provide some escape from the seemingly harsh words of Jesus. Recognizing the true meaning of the verb *orgizesthai*, however, allows us to realize that Jesus was not calling attention to *every experience of anger* or to our capacity for anger, but to the devastating results of anger that goes unresolved.

The Lists of Vices

Many other passages also refer to anger that has "gone bad." The Hebrew and Greek words for anger, or that refer to anger, do not indicate whether the anger is positive or negative. Whether the authors are referring to anger that is a normal response to threat or to anger that has become destructive depends on the context. For example, the same root word for anger is used to describe both Jesus' righteous anger at the Pharisees in Mark 3:5 and the selfish anger of the elder brother in the Prodigal Son parable in Luke 15:28.

This also helps us understand why anger is included in many lists of virtues and vices that appear in both ancient Mediterranean literature and the New Testament. In his list of vices, Paul borrows from these other sources and then applies them specifically to teaching the Christian communities which positive traits (virtues) to develop and which negative traits (vices) to avoid. Note the place of anger in the following lists:

> Now the works of the flesh are obvious: fornication, impurity, licentiousness, idolatry, sorcery, enmities, strife, jealousy, anger, quarrels, dissentions, factions, envy, drunkenness, carousing, and things like these. I am warning you, as I warned you before: those who do such things will not inherit the kingdom of God.
>
> (Gal. 5:19–21)

> For I fear that when I come, I may find you not as I wish . . . I fear that there may perhaps be quarreling, jealousy, anger, selfishness, slander, gossip, conceit, and disorder.
>
> (2 Cor. 12:20)

> But now you must get rid of all such things—anger, wrath, malice, slander, and abusive language from your mouth.
>
> (Col. 3:8)

> Put away from you all bitterness and wrath and anger and wrangling and slander, together with all malice.
>
> (Eph. 4:31)

It is easy to conclude from these lists that anger is always negative, and in fact these verses have been used to argue that all anger is sinful. But these lists do not exist in isolation; they are set over against the virtuous traits such as "love, joy, peace, patience, kindness, generosity, faithfulness, gentleness, and self-control" (Gal. 5:22–23), which Paul calls the "fruit of the Spirit." So given the list of surrounding words, it is obvious that the authors are describing anger that has "gone bad" and is expressed in ways that are life-destroying to both individuals and the community.

The anger mentioned in these lists is what happens when we forget to be "slow to anger," when we let the "sun go down on our anger and give opportunity to the devil." It is what happens to anger when we do not master the "sin lurking outside the door" of our hearts and minds. The problem Paul was addressing by including anger in these lists was not that the people in the churches were angry, but that Christians were *sinning* with their anger—being spiteful, bitter, and jealous, and calling names, spreading rumors, withdrawing, and so forth.

These lists of vices do not address our capacity for anger, nor every expression of anger, but only those forms of anger that cause hurt and alienation within the Christian community. And all of us know people who have been hurt in our church because of the pain they experienced from anger that had "gone bad."

CONCLUDING REFLECTIONS

So what conclusions does the Bible make about human anger? What can we as Christians learn about this powerful emotion from Scripture? I suggest the following theological ideas for your reflection.

You can see that the biblical stories and sayings described above *assume* that people experience anger. Scripture confirms that the *capacity for anger* is part of being human and *not a distortion of God's original creation*. Cain's capacity for anger was not a problem to God; Cain's *action* was the problem. Neither God nor Jesus ever suggests that good people never feel anger. The Ten Commandments contain no prohibition of anger, only of killing—a behavior that results from anger that is expressed destructively. Ephesians, in fact, commands Christians to identify and deal with their anger creatively before it can become destructive. The biblical material focuses on our accountability for *why* we are angry and *how we express* the anger. At no point does Scripture argue that the *capacity* for anger is evil and should be eradicated.

The Bible does not contradict what science and psychology have learned about anger. Rather these biblical stories confirm the same biological reality about our capacity for anger that we discussed in the last chapter—it is part of our very being, with us from the beginning, part of how God created us. Indeed, this capacity for anger is part of being created in the image of God, an idea that we will return to in the next chapter.

At the same time, we have to ask, Are the stories and sayings in Scripture concerned about anger? Definitely! It is obvious in both the Old and New Testaments that anger can lead to sin, and stories throughout the Bible criticize destructive expressions of anger. The story of Cain's murder of Abel is only the first in a long line of stories that chronicle the destructive powers of anger. The Bible is constantly asking readers to put away all expressions of anger that lead to pain and suffering. These stories confirm our own negative experience with anger, yet we must resist the temptation to conclude that anger is always a "deadly sin."

Scripture is clear, however, that when anger does lead to suffering, it *is not because anger itself is automatically bad,* but because the anger is either unnecessary or expressed harmfully. Like any aspect of life, the capacity for anger can be co-opted by sin and evil. As we have seen, Scripture is clearly aware of how the experience of anger makes us vulnerable to destructive, sinful behavior against our neighbors and ourselves. You and I are no exceptions; we have sinned with our anger. But that does not mean we have sinned every time we feel this emotion. To *feel* anger is not the same as sinning. *Why* we feel angry, and what we *do* with our anger addresses the moral questions. In fact, later chapters will describe how and when feeling angry is the right and loving response for Christians.

Now we move to another question: What does the Bible teach us about the anger of Jesus and God?

4

Did Jesus Get Angry?
(And What about God?)

Discussing what the Bible says about human anger is one thing, but searching for what it says about the anger of Jesus and God is a more difficult task. Before you read further, you might want to pause and ask yourself what you now believe about God and Jesus in relation to anger. Do you think Jesus ever got angry? That God feels anger? And what would their anger look like? Do your answers affect your thoughts about your own anger?

THE ANGER OF JESUS

Let's start with Jesus, the central character in our Christian faith, the One sent to bring a deeper understanding of, and connection with, the Creator. A core belief of the Christian tradition is that Jesus, in a manner far beyond our capacity to understand, was both fully human and fully divine. Jesus is our model for living a faithful life, so what can we learn from his life about anger?

Jesus, a Man with Emotions

First, we must note that Jesus is portrayed throughout the Gospels and the New Testament as a person with a full range of emotion. Jesus is described in these stories as a real person who can "sympathize with our weaknesses" because he "in every respect has been tested as we are" (Heb. 4:15). Jesus experienced and expressed sorrow as he overlooked the city of Jerusalem (Luke 19:41); he experienced fear in the Garden (Matt. 26:37–44); he felt grief at the tomb of Lazarus (John 11:35); he experienced joy in welcoming the children (Mark 10:16); and he felt disappointment in the denial of Peter (Luke 22:61).

Jesus' anxiety when he went into Gethsemane to pray is clearly described in the Gospels. Feel the fear in his request that God "remove this cup from me" (Mark 14:36). According to Matthew, he was "grieved and agitated" (Matt. 26:37); Mark notes that he was "distressed and agitated" (Mark 14:33); and Luke describes him in such "anguish" that "his sweat became like great drops of blood falling down on the ground" (Luke 22:44). Who among us has not felt this kind of intense anxiety?

Jesus also felt love, and it was probably the strongest emotion he expressed. The phrase "moved with compassion" is used in the Gospels only about Jesus or God.[1] The Greek word translated with this phrase indicates an intense physiological response. It refers to the part of our body where we most "feel" emotion, what we might call our "guts"—as in our statements such as "I felt like I had been kicked in the gut!" When Jesus felt compassion, it was a deep, powerful feeling rather than superficial sympathy. You will see in the following Gospel stories that Jesus' compassionate love is significantly related to his anger.

Anger at the Legalists

The Gospel of Mark reports that Jesus was angry when he confronted the Pharisees concerning whether or not it was appropriate to heal on the Sabbath.

Again he entered the synagogue, and a man was there who had a withered hand. They watched him to see whether he would cure him on the sabbath, so that they might accuse him. And he said to the man who had the withered hand, "Come forward." Then he said to them, "Is it lawful to do good or to do harm on the sabbath, to save life or to kill?" But they were silent. He looked around at them with anger; he was grieved at their hardness of heart and said to the man, "Stretch out your hand." He stretched it out, and his hand was restored.

(Mark 3:1–5)

No question here about what was going on inside Jesus as he looked around at the Pharisees. When Mark describes the emotion Jesus was feeling, he uses the Greek word *orge*—the word for anger most commonly used in the New Testament. It cannot be translated as any other emotion.

If Jesus was angry, then how could the experience of anger be considered a sin? If Jesus was able to live out his life in obedience to the will of God, to be "without sin," and if Mark's Gospel is an accurate witness, then we cannot consider every instance of anger sinful. Obviously other criteria must be used to label a particular experience of anger as sinful.

Indignation on Behalf of the Children

Jesus became angry with his own disciples when they tried to keep people from bringing children into his presence. Remember this brief story from the Gospel of Mark:

People were bringing little children to him in order that he might touch them; and the disciples spoke sternly to them. But when Jesus saw this, he was indignant and said to them, "Let the little children come to me, do not stop them; for it is to such as these that the kingdom of God belongs."

(Mark 10:13–14)

When I think of this story, I imagine Jesus sitting on a rock, resting against a small, scraggly tree. He has finished teaching, and children shyly gather around asking questions. At the same time, small children and infants (Luke 18:15) are being gently handed to him in order to receive his blessing, as was the custom of the day.

Suddenly, Jesus becomes aware of raised voices, and he hears his disciples rebuking the parents, aunts, uncles, and grandparents who are bringing the children to him, ordering them to keep the children away. When Jesus realizes what is happening, he is "indignant." The Greek word translated "indignant" is a highly charged word and means that Jesus was annoyed and irritated at his disciples.

The Bible speaks often of God's anger toward those who hurt their fellow human beings. Jesus' words about children's faith and humbleness in Matthew's Gospel are followed by this comment,

> "Whoever becomes humble like this child is the greatest in the kingdom of heaven. Whoever welcomes one such child in my name welcomes me. If any of you put a stumbling block before one of these little ones who believe in me, it would be better for you if a great millstone were fastened around your neck and you were drowned in the depth of the sea."
>
> (Matt. 18:5–6)

In other words, treat my children kindly, with goodness and mercy, or else! Can you sense the anger Jesus would feel toward anyone who did not treat children kindly or well? Or who hurt them and made them suffer?

Does it make you uncomfortable to think of Jesus the Christ being angry? Do you wonder whether Jesus was *that* human?

Eruption in the Temple

Read again the story about Jesus confronting the money changers in the temple. All four Gospels record this event, but we will use John's description.

The Passover of the Jews was near, and Jesus went up to Jerusalem. In the temple he found people selling cattle, sheep, and doves, and the money changers seated at their tables. Making a whip of cords, he drove all of them out of the temple, both the sheep and the cattle. He also poured out the coins of the money changers and overturned their tables. He told those who were selling the doves, "Take these things out of here! Stop making my Father's house a marketplace!"

(John 2:13–16)

Can you picture this wild scene? It must have been a chaotic few minutes that was burned into the disciples' minds. One passionate rabbi with a whip of cords suddenly moves against the establishment and drives them from the courtyard. Tables overturn with a crash, pigeons flutter loose, animals scatter, oxen bray, sheep bleat, coins clang and roll around the floor, people shout and dodge the whip, and gasps (and maybe some cheers?) escape from the stunned crowd. I doubt that Jesus hit anyone, but we must realize the explosiveness of his action. These people would not have been intimidated easily. The fury of his words and the strength of his physical presence moved them. The disciples were so amazed at his intensity they were reminded of the psalmist's words, "Zeal for your house will consume me" (John 2:17).

Can you read this story and doubt that Jesus was angry? Should it surprise us that Jesus would be indignant at these money changers who were making a mockery of worship, insulting God, and profiting from Jewish law? Many who read of this event in the life of Jesus *are* shocked. New Testament scholar Arthur Gossip says of this passage,

Desperate attempts have been made by some who feel uncomfortable over it to tone it down and edge out this incident . . . because they feel unhappily that it will not fit into their preconceived idea of what Christ should do and be; that here somehow he . . . lost his head and his temper.[2]

You may have had your own doubts about this passage. If you believe that Christians should not allow themselves to feel anger (or should not express it if they do), then you will certainly try to explain this event in some other way.

Words from the Cross

What do you think Jesus was feeling on the cross? In the Garden he had asked God to "remove this cup" if possible. He had already suffered the lashes and the crown of thorns at the hands of the Roman soldiers. He had been nailed cruelly to the cross. Surely he must have been threatened by the possibility that his whole mission had gone down the drain.

And where was God? Here at the end Jesus must have realized that there was no legion of angels coming to the rescue. Death was really happening. As a human being, Jesus must have felt deserted by the One he called "daddy." The coming of an untimely death provides a significant threat. And in response to this threat Jesus expressed anger at being abandoned, along with fear, when he "cried out with a loud voice, . . . 'My God, my God, why have you forsaken me?' " (Mark 15:34; Matt. 27:46).

Other Experiences of Anger

As you read the Gospels, notice other times when Jesus was probably angry. Doesn't he sound indignant when he tells Herod's messenger, "Go and tell that fox . . ." (Luke 13:32)? Doesn't he sound irritated when he calls the Pharisees "whitewashed tombs," "snakes," and "vipers" (Matt. 23:27, 33)? Doesn't the term "rebuke" describing Jesus' confrontation with unclean spirits (Mark 1:25, 5:8) suggest that he was angry at their destructive behavior? Even Peter, one of his most trusted disciples, caught an angry response when Jesus rebuked him with the words, "Get behind me, Satan!" (Matt. 16:23).

For Today's Christian

Several theological ideas that are central to the Christian tradition support the fact that Jesus felt emotions, including anger. First is the belief that Jesus, Son of God, was fully human. If you agree with most Christians that Jesus was fully incarnated ("God with us," as we celebrate during Advent), then it would follow that he experienced all the emotions that come with the territory of being human. From a biological perspective, incarnation means that Jesus had the same neurological warning system that we have—including the capacity for fear and anger.

Second, the man from Galilee was also like the rest of us in having clear values, beliefs, and meanings in his life. And like everyone of us, Jesus found himself in many circumstances in which these values, beliefs, and meanings were threatened. And when threatened, Jesus became angry. As the "threat model" describes, his neurological capacity for anger was activated in the temple, with the Pharisees, by the disciples over keeping the children away, and on the cross. If Jesus serves as our model for being fully human, shouldn't we, too, feel comfortable with our capacity for anger?

Most Christians think of Jesus as a model for living a faithful, God-centered life. Doesn't Jesus' example demand that we take more ethical responsibility with our anger, more action on behalf of those who are victimized? Most of the time we live in circumstances that call for conventional politeness and political correctness. But our weak faith, fear of anger, and lack of courage often hinder us when we should confront evil in the world as Jesus did.

DOES GOD GET ANGRY?

It is one thing to establish that Jesus experienced emotion, specifically anger, but what about God? Does God feel emotions, even anger? Christian scholars have wrestled with this question over the centuries,[3] but there is little doubt about the biblical perspective. Both the ancient Hebrews and the early Christians experienced God as a Personal Being with whom they could have a relationship, so they assigned personal characteristics to God—including emotions.

Biblical stories specifically describe God as having the capacity for experiencing anger and the willingness to express it. The Hebrew Bible frequently refers to specific instances when "the anger of the Lord was kindled against Israel" (Judg. 2:14). Jeremiah hears God discuss the idolatry of the people and proclaim that these actions "provoke me to anger." And then God says "My anger . . . will burn and not be quenched" (7:18, 20). The Israelites ask for mercy when God's anger is directed at them: "O LORD, do not rebuke me in your anger, or discipline me in your wrath" (Ps. 6:1).

References to God's anger in the New Testament are less numerous and less obvious. A story in the Letter to the Hebrews reminds readers that God had been angry at the Israelites who followed Moses out of Egypt. The author urges the brothers and sisters not to "have an evil, unbelieving heart that turns away from the living God" in order that they may avoid getting in the same situation as the Israelites "with whom [God] was . . . angry forty years" (3:12, 17). The Israelites believed that God could be provoked to anger by "an evil, unbelieving heart," "the deceitfulness of sin," "hardened hearts," disobedience, and rebelliousness (3:11–18).

We can also find support for the idea of God's anger (and emotion in general) in the way Jesus was related to God. When Philip asked Jesus what God is really like and the disciples asked Jesus to show them the Father, the answer from Jesus was, "He who has seen me has seen the Father." If you believe that Jesus was not only fully human, but in some mysterious way also fully divine (the Son of God, a member of the Godhead, one person of the Trinity), then it makes sense that since Jesus felt anger, then God must also feel anger.

God's Anger Is Rooted in Love

Why would God get angry? From a faith perspective, the answer begins in the context of God's most fundamental character trait: love. Steadfast love is a fundamental aspect of God's character:

But the steadfast love of the LORD is from everlasting to
   everlasting
on those who fear him.

(Ps. 103:17)

As a father has compassion for his children,
   So the LORD has compassion for those who fear him.

(Ps. 103:13)

God's desire to be in relationship with the creation, particularly
with us who are created in God's very image, is expressed as
desire for our well-being. God is quoted by Jeremiah as saying,

For surely I know the plans I have for you, says the LORD,
plans for your welfare and not for harm, to give you a future
with hope.

(Jer. 29:11)

Isaiah speaks of how God's love is expressed through grace and
mercy:

Therefore the LORD waits to be gracious to you;
therefore he will rise up to show mercy to you.
For the LORD is a God of justice;
blessed are all those who wait for him.

(Isa. 30:18)

The psalmist notes that gentleness and compassion are two
characteristics of love that guide God's anger. Love keeps God's
anger from being either spontaneously violent or chronically
bitter.

Yahweh is tender and compassionate,
slow to anger, most loving;
his indignation does not last forever,
his resentment exists a short time only.

(Ps. 103:8–9 *JB*)

The New Testament also identifies love as God's most basic
characteristic, an understanding that John puts very concisely

when he says, "God is love" (1 John 4:8). This all-encompassing aspect of God's nature is the motivation for God's emotional and behavioral responses toward creation. Moreover, as John noted, it was because "God so loved the world that he gave his only Son" (3:16), and the incarnation, God's coming to be with us in Jesus Christ, demonstrated how deeply God cares for us.

God is often pictured in the Bible as a passionate Being, characterized primarily by compassion for the poor, the dispossessed, the displaced, and those victimized by the rich and powerful. Noted New Testament scholar Marcus Borg argues persuasively that the concept of *compassion* sums up Jesus' teachings about God, for it describes an intense love expressed in action "on behalf of" the loved one. One succinct but powerful saying of Jesus sums up this truth: "Be compassionate as God is compassionate" (Luke 6:36).[4] So Jesus claims that God not only feels, but feels intensely! These words of Jesus challenge any idea that God is uninvolved, indifferent, or nonemotional. Rather, Jesus teaches that God has strong feelings about what happens in God's creation.

Can God Be Threatened?

I described in chapter 2 how anger occurs in response to a threat to ourselves. Can this "threat model" understanding of anger offer any insight into God's anger? Can God feel threatened? This idea sounded weird to me at first, because the idea of God being threatened suggests weakness. We don't like to think of God as vulnerable. But then we remember that love by its very nature is vulnerable to being threatened when those we love are hurt, rejected, ridiculed, or treated unjustly. From our personal experiences of loving we know that love always carries within it a certain vulnerability. We are heavily invested in those we love and may feel angered if something threatens a person we love or our relationship with that person.

Let's look at this issue from the perspective of how we respond when our values and commitments are trampled upon and see if we can draw any parallels with God's anger. The Judeo-Christian tradition believes that God is committed to specific values and desires for the creation: love and respect for each other, taking care of the environment, meeting the needs of the poor, and so forth. Christians have argued from the beginning that God has consistent covenants, grounded in steadfast love, that both inform and are reflected in God's actions and relationships.

It seems clear from a biblical perspective that at least two situations displease God: injustice and unnecessary suffering. The prophet Micah reminds his congregation of God's real desire: "what does the LORD require of you but to do justice, and to love kindness, and to walk humbly with your God?" (6:8). The "teaching of our God," says the prophet Isaiah, is to "seek justice, rescue the oppressed, defend the orphan, plead for the widow" (1:10, 17). The prophet Amos ties justice and righteousness together at the heart of God's expectations: "let justice roll down like waters, and righteousness like an ever-flowing stream" (5:24).

When we remember that God's basic character is love, we realize that God must be vulnerable and, therefore, can be threatened by human actions that harm God's beloved. Given God's passionate commitment to us, it is easy to imagine that when we behave in ways that hurt others, God feels threatened and responds in anger. So is God threatened by the genocide in Darfur, the innocent life lost in Iraq, the starving children in disadvantaged countries, the violence so prevalent in our culture, and so forth? Yes! God's love is invested in the victims of all these crimes against humanity. God desires for everyone to have abundant life, so God gets threatened by suffering and angry on behalf of the victims.

Love and Wrath

Some Christians emphasize God's wrath and use stories from the Old Testament to support the idea that when God's wrath is stirred up, it is expressed in ways that cause human suffering.

Pat Robertson, Jerry Falwell, and others believe that it was God's wrath that allowed the World Trade Center to be destroyed on 9/11 and that the 2004 tsunami was God's punishment on peoples that had persecuted Christians. They base their beliefs on certain stories in the Old Testament that portray God as a supporter of violence. To me this makes God a perpetrator, an immature parent who abuses nonobedient children. Contrary to this idea, I believe that God's anger is rooted in God's love, a love that expresses itself in ethical behavior, not in destructive action that causes more suffering. God's wrath is not a "thing" that stirs around in God's psyche like a raging lion, a loose cannon that God's love must constantly monitor. God doesn't have temper tantrums that destroy what God loves and wants to redeem. I do not believe that Scripture as a whole teaches us that wrath and love are two equal characteristics in God's nature. Rather, God's anger is subservient to love, a response of God's love to something going on in the world that is contrary to God's values.

I believe that the statement "God is love" (1 John 4:8) describes a foundational characteristic of God's being. Furthermore, I believe that the *capacity* for anger is an aspect of that love and is only triggered when God is threatened by human behaviors that are contrary to what God desires for the creation. I believe that *God's anger, therefore, is always an expression of God's love*. Rooted in compassion, it is always expressed in ultimately constructive ways.

For Today's Christian

So what does the link between God's anger and love have to do with regular human beings like us? When God first imagined bringing humans into being, God decided that they (male and female) would be constructed in the Creator's image (Gen. 1:26–27). This amazing idea is a central affirmation of the Christian understanding of humanity. In some mysterious manner we carry in our personhood the reflection (imperfect as it may be) of God's self. Therefore, since God feels emotions, including compassionate love and love's capacity for anger, then our emotions must be part of our "imageness." We believe that God is love, and that God's love gets angry, so it makes sense that we reflect God's capacity for both love and anger.

The Bible is clear that God becomes particularly angry in response to injustice and suffering. The psalmist says, "The LORD works vindication and justice for all who are oppressed" (Ps. 103:6). God's anger at that which causes brokenness at any point in the creation is an expression of anger in the service of love. This is poetically summarized in the words of C. S. Lewis, "Anger is the fluid that love bleeds when you cut it."[5] God's anger is not the *opposite* of God's love, but is experienced and expressed *because* of God's love.

Jesus, as the Son of God, reflected God's nature in his life and work. He loved others, and also became angry at injustice and radical suffering. When we let Jesus serve as the example of how we should live, we have yet another reason to understand that the capacity for anger is part of our personhood created in God's image. "For Jesus," says Marcus Borg, "compassion was the central quality of God and the central moral quality of a life centered in God."[6]

LOVING AS GOD LOVES: ANGER AT INJUSTICE

The reason you picked up this book is probably related to anger and conflict in close relationships with family and friends, and perhaps with neighbors, peers, and church members. In most of the book I focus on anger within these one-to-one relationships with people we know. However, what you have just read about the anger of Jesus and God can't help but make you aware of their anger on behalf of hurting people beyond our immediate circle of family, friends, and acquaintances. This book's subtitle, "Discovering Your Spiritual Ally," refers to anger as our ally on the larger stage of society as well. In chapter 7 we will talk specifically about the many ways in which our capacity for anger can be a spiritual ally, friend, and guide in living out the Christian faith, but let me spend a few paragraphs here examining the importance of anger in connection with peace and justice.

A significant point in Jesus' exclamation "Be compassionate as God is compassionate" is that we are invited, perhaps even challenged, to activate the emotions of love and anger as modeled after God. Because we are created in God's image, we have the capacity and privilege to love as God loves. If God's love can be threatened and God can become angry when any of God's beloved children are treated unjustly or suffer at the hands of others through violence, exploitation, poverty, prejudice, and greed, then the commandment "love your neighbor as yourself" actually means that sometimes our anger is the most loving response to the neighbor's situation. Shouldn't those of us who claim to know God feel this same compassionate anger at those situations, institutions, and people who cause the suffering and injustice?

What should we allow to make us angry on behalf of our neighbor? Together justice and righteousness refer to God's concern for the right of all persons—regardless of age, gender, race, religion, sexual orientation, and other distinctives—to be treated with respect, protected from oppression, and have their basic needs met by the community. Ideally, we have incorporated these values into our Christian faith so that decisions and actions that are unjust and cause suffering will violate our values. Anger becomes a spiritual ally when it allows us to adopt God's concerns about those who are neglected, or hurt, or hungry, or oppressed, or enslaved, or abused in any way by those in authority—particularly by the rich and powerful.

When situations occur in which injustice is obvious and radical suffering is evident, Christians *should* feel threatened and experience anger. Think of the suffering caused by intentional misbehavior on the part of another human being or institution: domestic abuse, rape, muggings, war, rejection, power politics, unsafe jobs, lies, road rage, incompetence, and abuse of the environment. If we are to love as God loves us, then it is obvious that we will become angry and take action. To be angry in the face of injustice and radical suffering is not a sin, but rather the mark of a person who is in fellowship with God, who has chosen to be on God's side against evil. Now, in light of what the Bible says, push this idea to the next level. From a Christian perspective *NOT being angry at evil, injustice, and suffering is sinful.*

Elie Wiesel, a Holocaust survivor, has said that God has given us an Eleventh Commandment: "Thou shalt not stand idly by." Wiesel connects righteous anger to moral action, saying, "I believe in compassionate anger!"[7] Compassionate anger inspired by love should motivate us to cry out for righteousness. We must realize that *not* to express our anger is, in effect, to collude with injustice, to support perpetrators through our silence.

In chapter 3 and this chapter, we have seen that the Bible agrees with scientific research; the Scriptures assume that the emotion of anger is a normal human response. Now we know that both Jesus and God felt this powerful emotion, and we have carefully related it to love. Scripture does not question our *capacity* for anger, but is concerned with anger's *destructive potential*—it offers many models for creative uses of anger. The Bible is not focused on eradicating the internal *experience* of anger, our capacity for anger, but on *why* we get angry and *how* to creatively handle the *expression* of anger. We even have the responsibility to express our anger when it is the loving thing to do. The next chapter will offer suggestions about how we can be responsible in dealing with our anger.

5

Dealing with Anger Creatively

Now what? You're back in your office after an intense meeting. You're seething inside about the way a colleague manipulated events and you're even angrier at your own inability to speak coherently in response. Or perhaps you remember last night when you yelled upstairs and angrily asked your spouse why she is always late. Or you are thinking about this morning when the children were goofing around at breakfast, and you told them to shut up.

When we are angry, it's common to blame our anger on another person or an institution. However, since our capacity for anger is only activated by our own interpretation that we are threatened, and since it is *our* values and beliefs that are threatened, we cannot hold others accountable for our anger. It is our responsibility to be accountable for *what* we feel angry about and *how* we express it.

Given that the capacity for anger is a gift from God for positive purposes, as Christians we must place primary responsibility for decisions about *what* to get angry about and *how* we express that anger squarely on our own shoulders. As persons created in the image of God, it is our privilege and responsibility to follow the advice of Ephesians: "Be angry, but do not sin."

You really want to handle your anger in ways that are life-enhancing for yourself, your family, and your community, rather than life-destroying. But how to do that?

In this chapter I present a constructive process that you, as an individual Christian, may use to help you handle anger more creatively and responsibly. It prevents us from doing harm with anger, and at the same time guides us in directing anger in the context of love—using its power for good rather than evil. The process has six steps:

1. Recognizing anger
2. Acknowledging anger
3. Calming our bodies
4. Understanding why we are threatened
5. Evaluating the validity of the threat
6. Communicating anger appropriately

STEP 1: RECOGNIZING ANGER

The first step in handling anger more creatively is *to increase your awareness* of your angry feelings. You may want to read this first sentence again. It contradicts the idea that good Christians should ignore or suppress experiences of anger. Denial and avoidance are constant temptations because of our fear of anger or of the power of the person or group with whom we are angry, or just because we don't want to spend the time and energy on the hassle. Avoiding anger for whatever reason, however, leads to denial and suppression, which are not the answer. Furthermore, when we suppress anger we deny an important aspect of the image of God reflected in us, and we refuse to accept one of God's gifts.

We cannot act responsibly with anger we don't recognize. Anger that is unidentified, or ignored, becomes even more dangerous. When we are not consciously aware of anger it is more likely to be expressed destructively than constructively. If you are a person who gets angry quickly and too often you express the anger before thinking, or you regularly express anger in disturbing and problematic ways, then you might think that increasing your ability to recognize anger is the last thing you need. The problem for you, however, is that you often don't recognize your anger in time to do something creative about it.

Fortunately for our discernment process, anger can't easily hide itself; it leaves clues to its presence in physical, mental, and behavioral signs. It's our responsibility to do the detective work necessary to identify these clues. What do we look for? You're probably familiar with all of them but perhaps just haven't linked them clearly to anger.

Anger, like all genuine emotion, expresses itself in our bodies, and if we pay attention anger will reveal itself through physical signs and symptoms that indicate that the body is becoming primed for flight or fight: grinding teeth, clenched fists, tight neck, cramping abdomen, and heart pumping. Although any number of other things may cause these physical symptoms, they are often signs that we are, or have been, angry.

Our moods can also reveal the presence of anger. Being grouchy, cranky, or "touchy" may indicate that we have been, or are, angry. The language that we and others use to describe our moods also provides clues—particularly synonyms for anger such as "irritated," "frustrated," "annoyed," "disappointed," "hurt," or "jealous." Using these words usually indicates that we have been threatened by some life circumstance.

Most of us can identify specific behaviors that are more likely to occur when we are sitting on, or not recognizing, our anger—nagging, hostile humor, abusive language, emotional games, alcohol abuse, overeating, depression, and the inability to sleep. More serious behavior includes acting violently by slapping, shaking, or punching a spouse, a child, or someone else. These are obvious clues and you should keep them in mind.

At least some of these behaviors might seem minor and be brushed off as irrelevant, but it is our responsibility to identify and deal with the anger in order to keep it from becoming more destructive. Being alert to such physical symptoms, moods, and behaviors may help us recognize anger early and allow us to deal with it more positively.

Pretending that anger doesn't exist increases the probability that it will do harm. When we ignore our angry feelings, we cannot discern why we are threatened, nor can we learn how to express anger appropriately. God gave us the power to reason, the power to choose, and the power to call on spiritual resources. But all of these are lost if we cannot acknowledge our anger. So a basic ethical principal for dealing with anger is that we are responsible for being aware of it and for keeping it conscious.

Finally, if you realize that you constantly suppress your anger, then discovering why you suppress it becomes an important step in learning to deal with anger creatively. Many personal issues can keep you from being conscious of your anger: a strong need to belong, the need to be in control, fear of retaliation, or concern that conflict will cause people to abandon you.

STEP 2: ACKNOWLEDGING ANGER

Once you recognize your anger, the next step is to acknowledge what you feel: to name it and claim it as yours. Naming something gives it an identity and makes it more difficult to brush aside or discount its significance. By acknowledging our anger we capture the reality of it by not allowing it to escape conscious awareness, and we confirm that dealing with it is our responsibility.

One problem in keeping anger conscious is that it often occurs at a time when it's impossible to deal with—minutes before company comes, just as your daughter must leave to catch the bus for school, as you arrive at church, or when an important long-distance call comes through. The adage "out of sight, out of mind" is very true. Because there is no time to reflect on, evaluate, or resolve it, we often forget the incident, ignore the emotional response, and move on with the day's schedule. By the end of the day, we have "forgotten" the situation that produced the anger. But our brain remembers, and when a similar situation occurs our anger will be more intense.

It becomes important, therefore, to capture the initial anger for further reflection and evaluation—to make a mental note to come back and attempt to resolve the issue. You can say something like:

— The Smiths have just pulled up so we can't discuss this now, but I'm angry that you didn't pick up the salads. We won't let it mess up the evening, but I really need to talk about it before we go to bed. Would you be willing to do that?

— I am really frustrated when you take so long to dress that you skip breakfast. When you get home from school let's talk, so we can understand each other better.

Acknowledging our anger before God is particularly important. Some people believe God gets upset at anger, and they want to hide their anger from God. But as with every other aspect of life, it is acceptable to share our anger with God. Placing our anger in the context of our faith makes it less likely we will deny or ignore it because the anger becomes an agenda item between God and us, and we can use our spiritual resources to deal with the anger event. This increases the probability that we will handle our anger wisely.

Asking God for help in learning from this event and for guidance in dealing with the anger constructively and not destructively is an appropriate prayer. Discussing our anger with God (1) names it, (2) acknowledges it, (3) asks for help in understanding the threat, and (4) commits us to dealing with it creatively. We may discover during this step of acknowledging our anger that the way we expressed our anger, verbally or behaviorally, hurt or harmed another person. Apologizing and asking for forgiveness may be appropriate.

STEP 3: CALMING THE BODY

Step 3 involves taking time to calm our bodies—to move from the physical readiness for fight or flight back to normal.

Remember the physical signs of anger: heart rate increases, muscles are contracted, blood flow adjusts, and blood chemistry changes. Why is this kind of physical arousal a problem? For several reasons. First, when these chemical and biological changes are not discharged by some intense physical fight or flight, they become destructive to our health—like any stress reaction. So learning how to calm our bodies and regain chemical balance is necessary in order to protect our health.

Second, when we're in a state of arousal we are more likely to overreact to other provocations and respond with words and actions we will later regret. Remember when you yelled unnecessarily at the children or your spouse, or barked harshly at a colleague, or drove too fast because you were still upset about a previous incident? Calming the body keeps us from making inappropriate angry responses at the wrong time and to the wrong people. And remember that stress of any sort keeps our bodies in a semi-aroused state, which makes us more vulnerable to becoming aroused and angry in situations that would not normally threaten us. One way to reduce your anger level is to keep stress to a minimum.

So how do you turn off the body's alarm system? One way you can bring your body chemistry back to neutral is by physical activity: cleaning the house, jogging, lifting weights, biking, walking, gardening, or working out on a stair-stepper or rowing machine. Or you may already have a favorite way of "calming" yourself: by listening to soothing music, playing an instrument, meditating, focused imagery, controlled deep breathing, repetition of a mantra, or other intentional ways of moving from this battle-ready condition to a state of relaxation. Many Christians also turn to prayer, in which they may practice "surrendering" the anger. Meditation may include images of biblical scenes that can bring a sense of security and peace. One person I know regularly used imagery from Psalm 23, envisioning being led into green pastures and beside still waters, as a way of calming down his body.

Using these practices to relieve tension *is not the same as suppressing anger*. Calming the body should not be an attempt to forget, avoid, or pretend we aren't angry. We are simply recognizing that our bodies have had an understandable physical response, rooted in our long biological history, which is not necessary for our survival in most situations today. Our mind is often aware of this before the body has figured it out. We are aware that a more creative response is possible if we calm our physical arousal. Our alarm system has mobilized us for fight or flight, but to preserve our health and to reduce the temptation to act irresponsibly, we need to relax.

STEP 4: UNDERSTANDING WHY WE ARE THREATENED

Another step in handling anger responsibly is to figure out *why* we are angry. Anger is an alarm system activated when one of our important values or beliefs is threatened. Remember that when Cain got angry, the first thing God asked was "Why are you angry?" (Gen. 4:6). God gave Cain a chance to understand why he was angry so that he might deal with it redemptively, which, sadly, Cain refused to do.

Until we understand the threat, we don't know whether our anger is valid—and requires action—or invalid, which means it is a problem that calls for a change in our personal values or beliefs.

Act like a detective. Ask yourself questions to guide your search: What was my anger all about? With whom am I angry? Why am I angry? What words, actions, insinuations, made me react? Which of my values, beliefs, expectations, or hopes feel ridiculed, attacked, or slandered? As you begin to answer these questions, you're engaging in self-assessment, working to gain insight so you can say "Oh, now I see why I am threatened." Let me illustrate with Brenda's experience.

Brenda, 34, was concerned about her intense emotional response to changes in her daughter's and her best friend's lives. Her older daughter, Lisa, a college student, had chosen to work at a national park rather than come home for the summer. When Lisa told her mother about her summer plans, Brenda became angry, and then later became "short and curt" with her husband for encouraging Lisa. Her anger continued to leak out. A few days later, to her surprise, she spoke an "ugly, angry jab" at her younger daughter, a junior in high school: "I suppose you'll run off to another state when you get out of high school too!" Having raised her children to be independent and make their own decisions, she was surprised at her anger.

That same week, her best friend, Cheryl, announced that she would be moving because her husband was changing jobs. Brenda immediately became angry with Cheryl and Cheryl's husband. She accused the husband of being insensitive to Cheryl and was angry with Cheryl for "not resisting this insensitive command." Her anger forced Cheryl to come to his defense, and her comments caused tension between the two women. Upon reflection, Brenda realized that her anger had blocked her from carefully listening to her friend. Cheryl was indeed excited about this move because it would take them near her family.

In our conversations, we raised two questions: how was she threatened and what stories (values, beliefs, and meanings) were under attack? Brenda recognized that she felt "deserted" in both instances. She felt that her daughter and her friend were "purposefully leaving her." She remembered angrily telling her husband that Cheryl must not be concerned about their friendship or she wouldn't be so happy about the move. She also recalled the "sinking feeling that Lisa didn't want to come home because of me." She went on to say, "I know they care about me, but my heart wonders why they would leave."

Exploring her own history for experiences of being "left," Brenda noted that she was adopted as a two-month-old. She had long been angry with her biological mother for "giving up on me." Brenda said with strong emotion, "She didn't even know me, but decided I wasn't worth keeping!" This intense mix of sadness and anger is a common response to "relinquishment," but Brenda had never been willing to verbalize this to another person. It's very difficult for people to verbalize old hurts, so Brenda was not unusual. She eventually rationalized that it was unfair to feel this way toward her birth mother when she didn't know all the circumstances.

It was relatively easy to identify the memories and personal stories that led to Brenda's strong reactions. She recognized fairly quickly that her anger contradicted her conscious values and created unnecessary tension in two important relationships. Her willingness to get assistance in understanding where her anger came from enabled her to identify a significant story that she had created about her adoption. She named the story "If you love me, you won't leave me" and summarized it with these words: "something is wrong with me that makes people give up on me and leave." Being able to talk about it and sharing it with another person—and later with both her daughter and her friend—allowed her to move ahead in handling her anger creatively.

When trying to understand what personal beliefs are threatened by a particular life situation, it is important to look for more than one. Behind many experiences of anger lie threats to multiple beliefs, and frequently one or more of our values are buried down inside our minds and hearts. It is fruitful to ask, "What other stories might be threatened?"

Jonathan and Susan, a newly married couple, were frustrated by their anger. Jonathan described a recent Sunday morning when he was angry with his wife because they were late to church again. After exploring many possibilities, Jonathan identified that one of his important values was "to be responsible." Being responsible included his belief that responsible people are on time. Furthermore, "being on time" for Jonathan means being in your seat a few minutes before the event starts. Susan also likes to be responsible, but for her "being on time" means getting there "before the main event is underway," because, as she says, "nothing starts on time anyway and the warm-up stuff isn't worth sitting through."

Their clash of values about the definition of "being on time" often caused conflict about departure times and, when they are late, Jonathan is threatened because he feels irresponsible. He angrily blames Susan for being irresponsible, and she gets angry in return because, she says, he has "assassinated my character!"

Why was there so much intensity around an important, but not unsolvable problem? To the question, "What other values could there be underneath all this?" Jonathan was able to discern a deeper threat. The clue came when he said that he felt "that she doesn't care for me" when she made them late. Since they had been married for almost a year, he believed that "she should know by now how important it is to me to be on time." When she didn't make the effort to be on time, a deeper value was threatened, which he described as "people who love each other behave in ways that help their partner accomplish goals and feel good about themselves." He found it "not very loving" that she didn't behave in a way that helped him feel this way.

Jonathan expected that people who love each other assist each other, especially in those activities that represent their basic personality. Being on time may seem like an insignificant value, but for Jonathan not only did it define in part who he was—a responsible person—it was surrounded by a more important value: love. Though Jonathan didn't like to be late, it was his more basic interpretation of Susan's behavior as "unloving" that was most threatening. Uncovering this deeper threat moved Jonathan and Susan to a more thorough assessment of their conflict.

As you can see from these examples, we can use anger as a "diagnostic window" to help us learn things about ourselves that help us move toward spiritual maturity. It was necessary for Brenda, Jonathan, and Susan to identify the deeper threats in order to begin a responsible process of handling conflict.

What about you? Do you have any ongoing angers, angers that consistently pop up in certain situations or with certain people?

STEP 5: EVALUATING THE VALIDITY OF THE THREAT

Some threats, of course, are legitimate and anger is an appropriate response. It is legitimate for Christians to be threatened by real physical, social, or relational dangers. Furthermore, in the last chapter we discussed those life circumstances that *should* threaten our Christian values.

Once we know why we feel threatened, we must figure out whether feeling threatened is necessary and appropriate. So the next question is "Did I need to be threatened?" Ideally the answer is based on those values and meanings that reflect our understanding of the Christian faith and its claims on our life. We can ask whether it is necessary for a maturing Christian to be threatened by that particular life circumstance. How does our understanding of what God expects of us contribute to this assessment? What would Christian love lead us to think about this value that has been threatened? Does it square with the model Jesus set for us? Does it reflect the "fruit of the Spirit" found in Galatians 5:22?

From the perspective of our spiritual journey we can identify which persons and events do not *have* to threaten us. As a person growing in grace, who is trying to love God and neighbor as self, we can begin to identify those life events that do not have to be *perceived* as a threat. When we do this, we often find that many of those things that threaten us are selfish, or culturally determined. On the basis of spiritual criteria we will be able to reduce unnecessary threats and, therefore, the amount of anger we experience. Let's return to Brenda's situation to illustrate.

Brenda's story about being given away because something was wrong with her leaves her particularly vulnerable to life events that make her feel she is being abandoned—relinquished yet again! Long-standing questions about her worth are raised automatically when people "leave" her. When she became aware of her story and her beliefs, and made the connections between them and her behavior, she was able to realize that the story under threat was not a valid story. The actions of her daughter and friend were in no way an indication that they loved her any less.

She was able to realize that the story she developed as a child, namely that her mother "must have known something about me" that made her "not want to keep me," was, as she called it, "irrational." She acknowledged that many other circumstances could have gone into that decision and decided to begin the process of finding out more about her birth family.

So Brenda was able to decide that those "stories" she had developed to explain why her mother gave her away were not realistic. She began to consider other possibilities, such as her mother's desire to give her a better life. Therefore, she didn't have to be threatened by being given up for adoption, but most important, she could stop being threatened when people "left" her for good reasons that had nothing to do with their love of her.

STEP 6: COMMUNICATING ANGER APPROPRIATELY

In most cases anger must be resolved if a relationship is to continue at the same level of mutuality, support, and friendship. If it isn't, reconciliation between you and a spouse, parent, child, friend, or colleague is difficult, and the continuing conflict and resentment can bring separation and alienation rather than love and genuine fellowship.

To resolve your anger you must first choose to communicate it, and then continue by describing what you have learned about the threat. Doing this invites the other person into a discussion that can lead to changes in how you understand each other and changes in behaviors that can reduce the threat.

Handling anger responsibly means expressing it in ways that don't wound or harm others. There's almost no way to predict when we'll let someone know we're angry. We might express our anger as soon as we feel it, immediately after something that

threatens us is said or done and before we have had an opportunity to think about it. Our quick anger can be verbal—"You
idiot, why did you say that?"—or nonverbal—we walk quickly
out of the room and slam the door. But these are not creative
ways of expressing anger, and when we are at our best we recognize their inappropriateness and childishness. The best thing
to do is to apologize for our harsh words or gestures and then
begin a more effective communication of our anger.

At other times we don't recognize our anger until later, perhaps when we become tense and suddenly find ourselves irritated with an innocent friend or family member for no good
reason. Eventually we realize that we're actually angry about
something that happened earlier, something said or not said,
done or not done—in a committee meeting, a phone call with
a friend, being stopped by a policeman, or being stuck in traffic.

Communicating anger is not easy, in large part because it
requires an honest conversation—and that can be hard. There
are three ways to go about having that conversation and attempt-
ing to resolve the issues: (1) The most obvious option is to communicate directly with the people or group that have threatened
us. (2) When direct one-on-one communication isn't a good
option, enlisting the help of a second party may help resolve
problems. (3) In other circumstances, however, expressing even
mild anger may be dangerous or impossible, so sharing the anger
privately with a third party is the better option.

Expressing Anger Directly

The goal of this first step is to set up a process of communication during a neutral time, when feelings are not running high
and it's easier for both of you to be objective.

When we determine that our anger is indeed triggered by a
valid threat and, therefore, is appropriate, the next step is communicating that anger in an effective, life-enhancing way. This
is not easy. But as Christians we are instructed to "put away
falsehood" and "speak the truth" (Eph. 4:25), which means that

leaving others with the false impression that everything is all right between us is to misrepresent ourselves and act unethically. Jesus said, "you will know the truth, and the truth will make you free" (John 8:32).

When you talk about or describe anger, you run the risk of upsetting people, making them defensive, and straining relationships. But family and friends often sense when we are angry anyway. They recognize the clues in our facial expressions, our tone of voice, or our silence. So we might as well discuss the feeling. They may even provide the perfect opening by asking, "What's wrong?" or saying, "You're upset with that, aren't you?" People, particularly family and friends, are often more mature than we might give them credit for and can handle a thoughtful, nonaccusative discussion.

What would your conversation be like? How can you talk about your anger without making the other person defensive so that a fight is almost inevitable? There are actually a number of ways you can make your conversation more of a dialogue than a confrontation:

(1) Begin by *inviting* your child, parent, spouse, or friend to talk with you. That is very important. Ask for some special time free from distractions and narrow time constraints. There are several ways to start. You may identify in your invitation that you want to talk about your anger: "I want to talk over the angry feelings we expressed yesterday before we left for work." Or you may want to wait until the other person has agreed to talk before you mention the subject: "I realize that I was angry when you decided to punish Lance the other day, and need to tell you what I was feeling."

You can also mention your desire to protect the relationship: "Our relationship is very important to me, and I feel terrible when conflict creates distance between us. The anger that popped up again this morning did that, and I'd like for us to try and understand it and do something about it. Would you join me?"

If you are concerned that you will be interrupted or challenged before you get a good start, and want to make sure that you can take responsibility for being nondefensive, you may say something like: "I might have trouble putting this into words; I would appreciate it if you would let me talk for a few minutes before you say anything."

I should note here that if you spoke or acted in some way that hurt this other person or damaged the relationship then an apology would be in order either before the invitation or before moving further into the conversation.

(2) Focus on what *you are feeling, not the behavior of the other person!* Too often our anger leads us to blame the other person for whatever the problem is. Conversations that begin with "You never think about . . . " or "That's just like you to . . ." or "Can't I ever count on you to . . ." and proceed to question the other person's integrity, common sense, or IQ rarely end in resolution or reconciliation!

The other person will be more comfortable if you concentrate on your response to the situation rather than their words or actions. Blaming and accusing someone makes them defensive and can cause an argument rather than a conversation—so the conflict becomes even more destructive.

(3) Take *responsibility* for your anger, which means remembering what you have learned about the "threat model." "Kelli, I know I'm feeling angry, and I've been trying to understand what threatens me. Let me describe it to you and see if it makes sense to you." You might even give a brief summary of what you know about the "threat model" to explain why you want to have this conversation. Your interest in understanding yourself communicates that you really are taking responsibility for your anger, rather than blaming, and lessens the other person's defensiveness.

(4) *Invite their perspective.* "Thanks for listening. I've described why I think *I* was threatened, and what seemed to be happening; tell me what was going on in your mind and what you thought was happening." When you ask for this, you're inviting the other person, without blame, to share her or his feelings and thoughts during the event. You will almost always learn something that you didn't know: a different perspective, a feeling you hadn't suspected, an insecurity you hadn't noticed.

If the other person was also angry, this can lead to understanding how he or she was threatened in the same situation.

(5) If your anger is with someone who knows you well, such as a spouse, parent, older child, or good friend, you can *request that they help you understand the anger.* "Honey, you know me well. Now that I've told you how I think I was threatened, tell me what other values, or needs, or beliefs of mine were threatened. What else do you think might have been going on?" This invites the person with whom you are angry to share in trying to sort out what happened, to join you as a teammate to investigate an angry situation. Your goal as a team is to make sense out of the anger, to uncover its source and seek a solution, rather than fighting to see who wins the battle. This approach makes your anger the focus of attention rather than each other, and further removes accusation or blame from the conversation.

(6) Because most of us try to avoid talking about or acknowledging our anger, it's not uncommon to let a frustrating situation occur over and over again without doing or saying anything. It can be a particular event in a relationship or even the ongoing behavior of the person that has angered you, but you didn't know how to approach the issue, or you expressed your anger ineffectively.

> Once again Ron was late to pick up their two boys, and Mandy was furious. When he finally arrived, she told him with a barely controlled fury that he "was never dependable, always irresponsible as a father," and he should never be surprised that she divorced him. Not surprisingly, he became defensive and responded by listing her shortcomings in a stinging rebuke.
>
> When she talked about the conversation with her divorce support group at church, they suggested a different type of communication. First they suggested that she try a letter to avoid his defensiveness, and then suggested how she could choose to communicate how she was threatened, since it had to do with the boys.
>
> So she did write a letter to Ron in which she apologized for "going off on him" and then tried to state her values and

why she got threatened when he was late. "When you did-n't show up on time again, this threatened my belief that when parents make a promise to children they should keep their word." She told him that the boys liked being with him and were always disappointed when their time with him was short-changed, and when they didn't receive any notes or presents from him on special occasions. She also described her hope that though they were divorced, the boys would learn important lessons from him as their father about keep-ing your word and being responsible.

Though Mandy's letter was never answered and never came up in conversation, her ex-husband did become more responsible in keeping his word to the boys. It was also important to her that she had expressed her anger more thoroughly and appro-priately, relieving some of her shame about "blowing up" at him so often. She continued to use this strategy of writing him let-ters when something was threatening about the relationship.

(7) Despite your best efforts to understand why you were threatened and feel angry, it is not always easy to understand your feelings. When you are angry but haven't got a clue as to why you are threatened, it is probably best to admit your inabil-ity to deal with your anger at the moment by saying: "I'm feel-ing frustrated/angry/upset, but am not sure exactly what is going on inside me." Then you can commit to deal with it later, which lets the other person know you are taking responsibility for your anger: "I don't want this to create distance between us and will let you know what I'm dealing with as soon as I begin to make sense of it." Or you can invite them to give you feed-back about their perceptions right away: "I'm not making sense of why I got angry at Mac at the party tonight; what do you think was happening?"

(8) *Reaching mutual understandings* is now possible. Hopefully the two of you will talk over the events that have sparked threat and anger, learning more about each other's experience. Values, needs, expectations, belief systems, and unique meanings will be named and evaluated. You will be seeking "shared meanings," that is, each working to understand how the other feels even

though you disagree about interpretations of the events that have led to the anger.[1] Differences can be noted and accepted. More conversations may be needed to give each person more time to think about deeper levels of threat. Third parties who know you both may be asked to help clarify what has occurred.

(9) When the nature of the threats becomes clear, then you and the other person can *begin to think of solutions*. Be careful not to decide too quickly on one solution. Take time to explore all of the possible behavioral changes that might reduce the threat to one or both parties. Often these solutions acknowledge new understandings of what each person feels and needs in the relationship. Sometimes different perspectives must simply be honored. But even in that circumstance, often covenants can be made that change behavior by one or both parties, reducing threats and, therefore, the anger.[2]

When you are angry at a group or institution—such as the leadership group at your church or the executive committee of a club—you might be able to ask for a face-to-face meeting in which you could communicate your anger and why you were threatened. At other times different strategies are necessary. If you are angry with some larger issue in the community, such as injustice in housing codes, or with state or federal government policy, you will probably have to write letters to congresspersons, or join groups who attempt to express anger at the systemic level in order to change attitudes and behaviors.

Using a Mediator or Consultant

What do you do when your anger is at a colleague at work, or a member of a club, or another member of a board on which you sit, or a parent of another swim team member? The direct approach described above can often be a first step in your efforts to resolve the problem. The person(s) might realize that there is a problem and be willing to participate in the type of communication described above.

But when that approach does not bring any resolution, then

inviting a mediator or consultant into a process of conflict resolution may provide a satisfactory solution. The process of
mediation can often facilitate more thorough and effective
communication, provide more complete insight and understanding, explore new possibilities for change, and lead to problem solving and reconciliation.

Jesus provides a model for dealing with our anger forth-
rightly, instructing us to take initiative in seeking reconciliation
with those with whom we are angry:

> If another member of the church sins against you, go and
> point out the fault when the two of you are alone. If the
> member listens to you, you have regained that one. But if
> you are not listened to, take one or two others along with
> you, so that every word may be confirmed by the evidence
> of two or three witnesses. If the member refuses to listen to
> them, tell it to the church.
>
> (Matt. 18:15–17)

What do you do, for example, when words and actions from
another person have clearly hurt, disrespected, harmed, or
wounded you—physically, socially, or spiritually? You try the
direct approach, but are laughed at, ignored, or discounted in
some way. Or if a person is expressing anger at you inappropri-
ately—for example, spreading rumors, writing nasty notes,
stalking you in some way—and your individual initiative does
not work, what then? You should quickly involve other people
in a type of confrontation called an intervention. In an intervention, several persons trusted by both you and the other person, meet together with both of you.

Delores was a staff member in a local church. A female
church member was making her uncomfortable; she was
e-mailing messages every day, writing her numerous notes,
and asking her inappropriate personal questions. She asked
Delores to become like a "sister" to her and always wanted
to sit by Delores in church and at church functions. Delores
became angry, but did not know how to deal with her anger

in an appropriate way and was fearful of causing alienation. She took her concern to the church personnel committee, who understood and appointed a subcommittee to meet with Delores and the church member to work out some understanding of appropriate boundaries. The conversation enabled the member to see that Delores could not be her "sister" because of her status as a staff member who needed to relate to every member equally.

In this situation, luckily, a healthy understanding was reached because the church member trusted the two members of the subcommittee who served as mediators. The church member chose to change her behavior and did not feel "put down" by the gentle confrontation.

You may find yourself as part of a group—such as a law firm, a church committee, a board of a nonprofit group, a homeowners co-op, or a neighborhood association—that suffers conflict over policy, personnel decisions, or use of funds, and people on both sides feel threatened. Such anger and conflict can cause serious divisions, hurt good friendships, move some people to leave the group, and even cause the demise of the organization. You may be able to invite the group to consider outside mediation, which can lead to a deeper level of communication, understanding the different perspectives, and finding options for compromise that had not been obvious.

Ralph was on the board of his church when the leadership group became divided about how to handle a staff problem. Lots of anger occurred among the factions—Ralph included. Ralph and two other members of this thirteen-person board convinced them to call in a mediator. A denominational mediator was asked to lead a retreat in which the board was led through a process of conflict management. Every person's angers were taken seriously, the various values and beliefs, particularly moral perspectives, were given full voice, and the threats identified. The group was able to resolve most of their differences, develop some protocols for the future that took the wide range of concerns seriously, and begin a process of acceptance of the diversity of opinions and experiences represented. Though two members resigned in protest, Ralph and the others felt good about the results and were aware that without mediation, a much more disastrous result was inevitable.

Mediation can also be used in individual situations, when people are unable to resolve differences that are creating anger and conflict. Spouses, parents and children, roommates, and other persons in special relationships may seek out a counselor to help them identify threats and reach effective covenants about behavioral change, or acceptance of differences, that allow them to restore their relationship.

Sharing Anger with a Trusted Other

Expressing anger directly to the person or institution is not always the most effective option, and it can be especially difficult if you are dependent on the relationship. Anger can be dangerous when expressed toward someone who has the power to hurt you emotionally, socially, financially, or physically—by divorcing, firing, giving a bad grade, or attacking with physical violence. You may fear, for example, that expressing anger toward an employer, a professor, a supervisor, a doctor, a spouse, or a parent could be perceived as an attack—or at least as disrespectful—and risk breaking the relationship or, even worse, sparking retribution or punishment.

In a situation like this, taking time to think through your feelings and then decide how to express the anger is often the wiser choice. When this happens, it can be helpful to find a person to talk to with whom you can share your anger. Another person can hear you speak out loud about the feelings you have, particularly the anger. They can encourage a complete unburdening of the many feelings that you have probably stuffed inside and can help you begin the process of uncovering the threats.

Expressing anger can also be difficult or dangerous if you are angry with someone over whom you have control. Suppose you have intense anger toward one of your children even though you are aware that the child's behavior is mostly related to the child's particular age and stage. You understand that to express anger at the child could be destructive.

> Lana and Howard came to see me because they were "always picking at each other and hurting each other with nasty comments." They didn't understand why they felt alienated from each other. As we talked, I learned that they have a four-year-old child, Eddie, who is developmentally challenged. Eddie was born with congenital birth defects that have impaired his physical coordination and his mental capacities. Eddie's needs are numerous. He does not always control his bowels and bladder. He gets very frustrated when his limited physical ability does not allow him to do what his friends or siblings can do. This frustration can generate temper tantrums. Since Eddie needs constant supervision, Lana and Howard must curtail their own work and leisure. Caring for Eddie has many rewards because he is very lovable. However, his limitations do lead to behavioral patterns and confinement that are threatening to Lana and Howard's goals and ideals for Eddie and for themselves. Occasionally, of course, this produces anger.

What are Lana and Howard to do with their anger? To express it directly toward Eddie would not be appropriate (except for the amount of anger Eddie needs to hear to help him learn limits to his behavior). Eddie is not responsible for his birth, his disabilities, or (at his age) his frustrations. But that doesn't keep Lana and Howard from feeling threatened and angry that they have a son whose presence limits their activity, demands much of their time, and threatens their goals. They know that "dumping" their anger on Eddie would be unethical. Instead, they feel bad about the anger, and both try to keep it hidden.

What happened is that each misplaced the anger on the other, feeling and expressing much more anger over little things than was necessary. Instead of allowing their mutual anger about Eddie's situation to be an external problem they shared, they "dumped" it on each other. That, of course, interrupted their own intimacy and the support that they needed from each other. In time, they learned to identify and then express their anger about Eddie to each other. But each also chose a trusted friend with whom to share the excess anger, and they joined a support group of parents in similar circumstances.

We may also need to share our anger with another person when the source of the threat is not available—because of death, age, mental health, or geography. It is not unusual to feel anger toward a person who is now dead for actions that hurt us emotionally or physically: a mother who deserted the family to marry another man, a father who was abusive, a drunk driver who caused the accident, or a brother who committed suicide. For Fredrick, his father's age meant it was inappropriate for him to communicate his anger directly:

> Fredrick admitted his intense anger toward his father for his unrelenting criticism of Fredrick's intellectual and physical abilities when he was an adolescent. After several conversations with his pastor, Fredrick could recognize the effects of this anger in his present relationships. Fredrick and his pastor considered how he could overcome the alienation that had characterized his relationship with his father for more than thirty years. He imagined expressing this anger directly to his father. However, his father was now in a nursing home in frail health, so Fredrick decided that it would not be a caring action to "dump all this old crap in my father's lap now." So he decided to express his anger by writing a long letter to his father and reading his words to this trusted pastor. The letter became part of his healing process and freed him to choose other behaviors that he hoped would communicate to his father, even in the nursing home, his desire for reconciliation.

If you are feeling anger about a past or present event or relationship but expressing that anger directly isn't wise or even possible, it is a good option to explore more thoroughly the causes and effects by sharing it with a trustworthy person. Find a pastor, priest, or therapist who is knowledgeable and competent in guiding an angry person through the processes described in these chapters. After listening to you, if this person doesn't feel competent, or have the time, to participate with you in this process, he or she will know persons in your community who are fully trained.

SEEKING A COUNSELOR

After examining your anger for many weeks and months, perhaps you are now able to identify why you feel threatened in many situations. However, in certain circumstances your anger makes no sense to you. Even when you work hard to discover the nature of a threat, no quick answers may emerge. When you ask, "Why did I get angry at that?" you cannot uncover a satisfactory answer.

Or perhaps you keep getting intensely angry over the same things. You know why you got angry, but you don't understand why the anger is so intense. What does this mean? It probably means that your anger is related to past events. Chronic anger may be related to specific traumatic events from the past, or it may be related to long-term relationships that, because of constant conflict, overdependence, or emotional abuse, continue to affect you today. In any case it is difficult to come to grips with anger from yesterday. This chronic anger may have been eating away at you for a long time. It has also been slowly poisoning you and your relationships.

So what next? I suggest that your next step is to see a counselor. No, I don't think you are crazy, but you do want help in becoming what God wants you to become. You want to grow, develop, and mature, but aren't making the headway you want with the anger issue. I know you are concerned about the long-range impact your anger is having on your spouse, children, and friends at work and church. Because you love them, and because you take seriously Paul's admonition, "Be angry, but do not sin" (Eph. 4:26), I know you would like to find out what is causing your anger so you can deal with it more effectively. Ask people such as your pastor, your physician, or your friends about competent counselors in your locality. They may be pastoral counselors, licensed professional counselors, psychologists, psychiatrists, social workers, or other mental health specialists. Make an appointment and tell the counselor that you are struggling with handling your anger more creatively and want help in accomplishing that goal.

6

Anger Can Be Destructive

I hope it is clear by now that the capacity for anger and fear is a normal part of human existence. It is a planned and important feature of God's created order, a necessary and potentially good part of our basic nature. If we did not feel anger (and fear) in the face of threats, including the physical readiness necessary to resist or escape danger, we humans would not have survived. They motivate action and behavior that enables us to defend against attacks on our selfhood. But *anger also has a dark side.*

Anger, like most good things in life—such as food, sex, and ambition—can be distorted and misused, becoming a vehicle of destruction. We are reminded every day of anger expressed explosively when we observe yelling, swearing, reckless driving, slamming doors, and temper tantrums, and we hear all too many reports of anger violently expressed in spouse and child abuse, muggings, rape, murder, drive-by shootings, suicide bombers, and armed rockets. We have seen the devastating results of such behavior on families, neighbors, communities, and nations. We are painfully aware of the suffering caused and the lives and relationships permanently altered or destroyed, by these expressions of anger.

Less obvious, however, is the hurt and anguish caused by anger that is communicated through subtle, yet poisonous, words and behaviors. I am talking about such things as sarcasm, nagging, silence, withdrawal, procrastination, sexual affairs, harsh sermons, and "looks that could kill." We can't deny their disastrous effect on relationships between family and friends. Many of us have been targets of such forms of distorted anger and know how it hurts us. Furthermore, when we are honest, we realize our anger has hurt others. We, too, have expressed our anger in some of these unhealthy and destructive ways.

Those who lack the freedom or courage to be open with their anger may use these backhanded, less obvious expressions of anger. These are the people of whom it has been said, "They don't get angry but they always get even." But often we use these destructive words and behaviors when we do not realize, or will not admit, that we are angry. Recognizing the dark side of anger is necessary to protect others and ourselves from anger "gone bad." We need to open our eyes and learn to identify these less obvious expressions of anger. Now I want to raise your awareness of the many ways anger hinders abundant life for both others and ourselves.

ANGER IN DISGUISE

When you imagine someone being angry, you may picture physical anger—yelling, throwing dishes, smashing doors, or driving recklessly. If so, you may find it difficult to recognize anger when it is disguised. Yet, much of the anger that people ignore, swallow, or push back into the closets of their mind will sneak out dressed in another costume.

How do you discover whether a particular behavior is actually camouflaged anger? The best way is to pay attention to the results of your behavior rather than to its superficial intentions. If your action, or lack of action, hurts, frustrates, embarrasses, or makes another person mad, it is probably anger. This kind of anger can show up in a variety of disguises, including hostile humor, nagging, silence, sexual behavior, and passive aggressive behavior.

Hostile Humor

Humor is a very common disguise for anger. Sarcasm is its most obvious form—its goal is to hurt through ridicule. Teasing and "kidding around" can be humorous and witty when everyone, including the one being teased, has fun. But sometimes the kidding around has a "bite" to it. Someone is "cut" or "put down" by the remarks. Everyone may still laugh, in an uncomfortable way, but people recognize that the real purpose of the humor was not to have fun *with* someone, but to embarrass or ridicule that person. Anger was the motive, whether recognized or not.

Married couples sometimes use hostile humor to express anger deviously. Have you ever focused people's laughter on your spouse in order to gain some measure of revenge? Hostile humor is usually used in social situations where it is difficult for the spouse to respond. If you have used social occasions for veiled expressions of anger, you will understand why you and your spouse felt distant and irritable with each other on the way home—and maybe someone slept on the couch.

Parents and adolescents in conflict also use hostile humor. Adolescents make fun of their "too old to know the score" parents, and the parents ridicule their adolescent's hair, clothes, music, language, and friends. Humor can be an effective expression of affection and create a sense of warmth and closeness. But when humor is used to express anger, it causes "coolness" and distance.

Nagging

It is important to feel that our loved ones pay attention to our thoughts and ideas. When this does not seem to be the case, we begin to feel both powerless to change their behavior and unloved because they fail to change what annoys us. To feel helpless is threatening and anger producing, particularly if the person you wish to influence represents an important relationship. If a parent, for example, feels powerless to change a child's behavior or does not feel adequate in the relationship, he or she may express anger through constant complaining.

Nagging is a fairly safe way to express anger, but it is also ineffective. Why do people do it? It is a low-risk, impotent display of anger. Nagging masquerades as "I'm only trying to help you" or "I'm just reminding you." In truth, it almost always reveals longstanding anger in response to the threat of powerlessness to change another's behavior and the sense of being unappreciated because of that ongoing behavior.

Silence and Withdrawal

Silence and withdrawal are two of the most common means by which we try to conceal anger, yet make sure our displeasure is known. My wife, Judy, and I used silence and withdrawal to express anger in the early years of our marriage. Both of us were uncomfortable with anger, so we denied and suppressed most of our angry feelings. We could not admit that we were angry, so we did not deal with the anger creatively.

> When Judy was angry she got intensely quiet. She could create silence so thick I could feel it in the air. Her silence threatened me because of my fears about anger and my assumption (at that time) that if she was angry with me, she must not love me. My response to this threat, of course, was to become angry. Because I considered it unchristian to get angry in return (which to me meant raising my voice or allowing my irritation to show), I withdrew. Sometimes I withdrew into a corner to read, but often 1 would find socially acceptable reasons to literally leave the apartment. Going to play ball or visiting the library (where I would pretend to study while I tried to figure out what was going on) were two ways to "leave" her. My leaving satisfied several

needs, although I was unaware of them at the time. First, I could get away from her anger, which was making me uncomfortable. Second, I could express my own anger by "punishing" her for being angry with me. I knew that my leaving upset her. When I was really angry and trying "to win" the battle, I would not come home until after the time when I knew she would go to bed because, as a teacher, she had to get up early. She really disliked going to bed alone, so my action said in effect, "If you are going to be angry and not talk to me, then I'll get back at you by not going to bed at the same time you do!"

As you can imagine, we did not experience much love and intimacy during these times of silence and withdrawal. Anger had become destructive to our marriage. The sad thing is that we did not know what was happening. We had not been taught how to deal with anger and conflict in a relationship. We later learned that anger is a natural occurrence in close relationships. Instead of being so afraid of our anger, we began to take the risk of sharing it with each other as we did other thoughts and feelings. We started taking responsibility for using anger constructively instead of allowing it to rob us of our happiness. We know now that anger has the potential for increasing intimacy in close relationships.

Sexual Misbehavior

Indirect expressions of hostility in social gatherings include partners who accomplish this through flirtation. If you and your partner are experiencing conflict in your relationship, you may choose to hurt your spouse through flirtation. If you are unaware of your hidden anger, you might not be aware that you are flirting to hurt your partner. If your partner accused you of trying to hurt him or her, you would probably deny that you intended to do so.

Withholding sex is another deceptive expression of anger that has probably been going on since Adam and Eve, and counselors often work with couples in which one or both partners are pouting by refusing sexual encounters. Refusing to help a person meet a basic need is often an indirect expression of hostility. Sexual fulfillment, of course, happens to be one of the most basic needs. Have you ever expressed your anger toward your partner by turning off sexually?

If flirtation or withholding sex become a standard method of expressing anger in a relationship, then either partner might escalate the battle by having an affair, which really hurts. As a marriage and family therapist, I work with many couples whose relationship has been disrupted, sometimes fatally wounded, by an affair. These affairs are often symptomatic of problems in the relationship rather than the cause of the problems.

Why do people have affairs? The answers vary: "for sexual fulfillment," "he listens to me," "because she understands me," "he treats me special," or "she shows interest in my work." What lies behind these comments? Oftentimes, the person having the affair had a long-standing anger with the partner, feeling that the partner was not interested in, or concerned about, these specific needs. When people's needs go unheard, and their anger is ignored, or when they cannot express anger directly, then affairs are a way of expressing the anger and taking revenge.

Passive Aggressive Behavior

Anger is sometimes disguised by behavior that the angry person calls something else, such as a mistake, good intentions, or a poor memory. Sometimes the anger is so suppressed that the person expressing the anger in one of these ways may consciously deny that the actions are motivated by anger. That is why these incidents are often followed by, "Gee, I'm so sorry." Psychologists call these behaviors "passive aggressive," indicating anger that is not clearly communicated by outward aggression or direct communication, but is nevertheless intended to make others uncomfortable. Passive aggression is basically a way of "getting even."

Have you ever been late, for example, and explained with, "I'm sorry, but I got held up." Upon further reflection, you might realize that you were actually "paying someone back" for some word or action that was threatening to you. Procrastinating can be a way of getting even. Saying, "Well, I intended to get that done today, but . . ." might be hiding your true feelings. You might really be feeling, "You don't deserve to have me do something for you today," or "If you hadn't been nasty to me yesterday, I wouldn't have minded doing that for you."

The same hostile message may be expressed by forgetting things. Forgetting, of course, is usually followed by a statement such as, "I'm so sorry, I don't know why I forgot to pick up the milk." The reason might lie in the unresolved conflict that took place that morning at the breakfast table. One spouse might say, "Did that check have to be deposited today? Oh my, I guess I made a mistake." Yes, she did, and the "mistake" made her husband angry, but it allowed her to deny that she was expressing her long-time anger at her husband over being left out of financial decisions.

MISDIRECTED ANGER

Anger also becomes destructive when it is directed at the wrong target: anger directed at your assistant when it was actually generated by your sister, for example, or at your teenager when the anger is left over from a meeting with your supervisor earlier in the day. "Dumping" anger on your assistant and your teenager when it belongs somewhere else is of course unjust. Not surprisingly, there are common scapegoats for misplaced anger, and we're all familiar with them.

Anger toward the Self

We are often the innocent victim of our own misplaced anger. Sometimes, instead of expressing anger toward the person or event that poses the real threat, we turn our anger toward ourselves. For example, you may feel quite angry with another person, but not want anyone to know you are angry. To protect your image as a nice, calm individual you might expend a lot of energy keeping this anger from spilling out onto others. What happens? The anger, like a stopped-up sewer, backs up until it spills over inside and poisons the self.

This self-poisoning is most obvious when the anger literally "attacks" your body and becomes physically destructive. Studies of the integral body-mind-emotion connection reveal that physical disorders that can be caused or aggravated by internalized anger include cardiovascular problems, gastrointestinal disorders, and many inflammatory disorders.

At other times we purposefully aim anger toward ourselves. You may accuse yourself of failures and inadequacies, particularly in response to feeling guilty or ashamed. Young women who cut themselves, for example, are often aiming anger at themselves. Other self-destructive behavior such as problem drinking, taking drugs, or reckless driving can also be an expression of anger at the self. When you hold yourself responsible for events that generate anger, either in other people or yourself, you may end up feeling worthless and undeserving.

Anger toward an Innocent Party

Misplaced anger also occurs when it is dumped on an innocent object or person. Cartoons abound depicting this little drama. Have you ever become angered at work, but instead of dealing with it there brought it home, where it wreaked havoc on the rest of the family? The family did not deserve it, but they became the victims anyway. The injustice felt by partners who serve as substitute targets contributes to the dysfunction and eventual breakup of many relationships. Untold numbers of children have carried into their adult lives a troublesome, deep-seated rage over the injustice they felt at being substitute targets for parental wrath.

Teens are often in situations where they are angry with others or themselves but cannot express those feelings. Parents make fairly safe targets. A fifteen-year-old daughter, for example, is ridiculed by peers for something she is wearing, then comes home and yells at her parents when they ask her to put the recycle cart out by the driveway. It's not easy for anyone, including a parent, to be the substitute target for anger that belongs somewhere else. When parents are at their best they can resist getting threatened and perhaps help a child or teenager identify the real source of threat.

We direct anger at substitute targets for many reasons. If the person who was the source of the threat is very powerful, such as the boss, a police officer, or an authoritarian parent, we may find it too risky to express anger directly toward him or her. Where do you dump it? Often on a scapegoat, such as your partner, child, a golf ball, or a door.

"Porcupine Syndrome"

Some people are constantly angry. They seem always on the verge of being mad. You would describe their daily life with words such as harsh, intolerant, demanding, quarrelsome, cruel, bitter, vengeful, and spiteful. They are people with whom you do not want to spend time because their anger is always leaking out. It is often disguised and usually misdirected. I call it the "porcupine syndrome" because if you get near them, you will get pricked.

These people relate angrily because they feel constantly threatened on every front. They perceive their selfhood to be under frequent attack. These people are basically insecure, and the underlying anxiety keeps them in a constant state of defensiveness. Their alarm system is stuck in the "on" position, keeping them mobilized for attack at any time. People rarely recognize the porcupine syndrome in themselves, but if you have any suspicions about yourself check with trusted family members and friends for their impressions! Ask them how they experience you when you get angry. Ask if they suspect that you get angry too often and at too many situations when it is unnecessary.

Explosive Anger

Anger becomes most obviously destructive when it explodes in brutal rage: shootings, beatings, rapes. Violence has always been a part of American culture (and most of human history). Whatever the root cause, violence is usually disastrous because of the damage done both to the victim and to the one who is violent. Reconciliation is rarely achieved by violence. When the Jews came to arrest Jesus in the Garden, Peter felt that his investment in Jesus and his mission were threatened. His angry response was to attack the slave of the high priest, cutting off the man's ear (John 18:10). Jesus, however, rebuked the disciple's use of violence (although, interestingly, he did not chastise him for feeling threatened and angry): "But Jesus said, 'No more of this!' And he touched his ear and healed him" (Luke 22:51). Matthew quotes Jesus in this same incident saying, "All who take the sword will perish by the sword" (Matt. 26:52).

Any opportunities we have to help control violence—by protesting the easy access to guns, by offering more help to teens in trouble, by monitoring media access to our children, by taking a stand against torture, and by joining groups that foster tolerance and educate the public in acceptance of the diversity among us—are ways in which we as Christians can protest against violence in our culture.

WHY ANGER GOES BAD

How does anger become corrupted in these many ways? What transforms anger from a potentially creative power into a devastating force—into bitterness, revenge, hostility, raging abuse, and hate?

Poor Models

One obvious answer is that many people grow up with poor models for handling anger. Think about significant adults in your past, and how you may have unwittingly followed bad models for how you handle anger.

I have already mentioned that one reason Judy and I mishandled our anger was the lack of good models. My parents did not deal with their anger in the open where the children could learn from careful, thoughtful working through of anger. But given the contrast with some of the destructive anger I witnessed in my extended family and in the homes of some of my friends, I liked my family's style and vowed to carry it into my own marriage. Judy's father, however, frightened her with his anger. Not liking the intimidation, she also vowed not to let this "hot-tempered" style appear in our marriage. So we knew how we were *not* going to handle our anger. Sadly, however, we had few clues from either family or our church about how to handle our anger creatively.

Children learn early to duplicate what they see happening in their family and in childcare situations. They learn about nagging, yelling, silence, withdrawal, verbal abuse, violence, and so forth. These ways of expressing anger may become their "default" response as adults. Does *what* you get angry at and *how* you express it copy an adult model from your history? Do you catch yourself being angry with your spouse or children in ways that remind you of your family of origin? Do you behave in ways you promised yourself back then you would not repeat?

Some people grow up in families or subcultures where violence is a way of life. They were battered and bruised in homes where physical or emotional abuse occurred regularly. When they get irritated or frustrated, these children are likely to respond with physical outbursts. Research shows that when these children become adults they are more likely to respond to threats in the same manner.

Other children are reared without limits and restrictions by parents who are afraid to discipline. These children may learn to use temper tantrums to control their parents. As adults they may continue to use explosive angry behavior (even when they are not really very threatened) to dominate and control others.

An important reason for Christians to learn more about anger, and how to handle it creatively, is to provide positive models for our children and friends. I hope this book will offer some different ways for you to understand and effectively deal with anger. We can change these patterns, but it is not easy. Once identified, however, the *reasons* you get threatened and the *behaviors* that express valid anger can be changed. A good counselor can help you accomplish new ways of coping.

Suppressed Anger

When anger is always assumed to be negative or destructive, people who want to be nice often fail to recognize or deal openly with their anger. If you have learned somehow that good Christians should not feel any anger, you may find it difficult to acknowledge your anger. Anger is so frightening to many Christians that when it does occur, they quickly try to forget it or pretend it was inconsequential or "hold it in." Believing that anger is one of the deadly sins may cause you to pretend you don't get angry. Or you may believe that loving others means that you shouldn't be angry with them. Or your fear of hurting someone with your anger can lead you to hide or "swallow" the anger. From there, the next step is to deny or suppress your anger, and this provides a context for anger to "go bad."

When we refuse to be aware of, pay attention to, or acknowledge angry feelings, then we are functioning in ways that psychologists call *denial* and *suppression*—a process of keeping anger out of our conscious minds. "Denial" describes a situation when anger happens, but the person does not allow conscious awareness of the angry emotion stirred up inside.

"Suppression" describes what happens when an angry emotional response is recognized but is so threatening (perhaps to our ideas about anger) that it is immediately pushed into the closets of our awareness.

What happens when we deny or suppress anger? The stories of the events that caused the threat and the anger are imprinted in our memory banks. The threats stay alive in the "back pockets" of our mind and heart where many of our experiences are kept out of sight. Thoughts and emotions that we keep hidden in these "out-of-sight, out-of-mind" places continue to affect who we are and what we do.

Some situations elicit more anger than you would expect. Can you recall such a situation? An incident that deserves minor irritation somehow generates a ton of intense hostile feelings. What happened? Where did the extra "heat" come from? Probably from the place in the brain where unexpressed, unresolved anger is buried and festers.

> The children had been washing the family car as a birthday present for dad. But in the process a window had been left open and water had gotten inside on the upholstery. When Dad, a military officer, got home from the base he at first appreciated the gesture, but when he saw that water had gotten into the car he exploded. He chastised the children for being careless and causing water damage to his car. He was so furious that he told them they had ruined his birthday and sent them to their rooms. His wife, as you can imagine, was very upset with his behavior and his failure to appreciate what their intentions were and the love they were trying to express.

Why was the dad so intensely angry? First, he had run afoul of the commanding officer at headquarters that day and been warned that a repeat would result in a poor report. So some of the anger he was unable to express at his commander spilled out on the children. Second, he was angry with himself for the careless mistake that had drawn the reprimand, but he didn't do well in expressing anger at himself, so that sparked additional "heat" toward the children. Third, he was a "neat freak" and was upset when the children didn't accomplish something up to his standards. Not only did water get in the car, but the car was not as clean as he expected. So instead of taking joy in the gift his young children were offering, his suppressed anger from other sources suddenly came blasting out at the children, and he "lost his temper."

What actually happens to anger from the past? All the answers are not known, but it is clear that anger felt in the past can exacerbate anger we feel in the present. It is not so much like a small pot of boiling anger residing in some corner of the psyche as it is like a psychic CD where our frustrations, irritations, and injustices from the past are recorded: the brain remembers. When a current situation strikes us as being similar to one of these past events, it prompts a "replay" process in which the previous anger is recalled. If that anger was not expressed effectively and creatively resolved, then the memory may evoke the same emotional response that occurred at the time of the original event. Our memories of unresolved anger often make the present anger much stronger (hotter!) than the present situation warrants.

> Linda gets furious at her husband, Richard, for not "paying attention" when she is talking, for not "noticing what I do," and for "taking me for granted." But she is aware that her anger toward him is usually undeserved. And when she reflects on their relationship, she describes Richard as a sensitive, thoughtful person who spends time with her, listens patiently, and compliments her work. "I know he loves me," she says tearfully. "Why do I get so angry?"
>
> Linda spent much of her childhood and teenage years trying to get the attention and approval of her father. He was a competent, respected physician. Linda admired him and was proud to be his daughter, but his schedule allowed little time for her. He was, furthermore, a perfectionist and often critical of Linda. Despite her efforts to get his attention and earn his approval, she rarely felt that she was important to him. This constantly frustrated and hurt her. By her teenage

years her anger toward him was strong, even though she rarely expressed it openly.

Somewhere in the back of her mind, Linda recorded these times when she could not get the attention and approval she wanted. Furthermore, her brain recorded the threat and anger she felt. Now when her husband gives the slightest hint of not paying full attention or giving complete approval, it reminds her inner self of this previous threat and anger. Because she is so vulnerable to this particular threat, her anger at her husband is exaggerated. Linda is working at recognizing and reconciling this old anger. First she had to become aware of how the old memories affect her current situation. Then she was able to separate yesterday's anger from today's anger.

I think the apostle Paul was speaking of this unseen feature of our human nature when he said, "I do not understand my own actions. For I do not do what I want, but I do the very thing I hate" (Rom. 7:15). He also became frustrated at actions that were contrary to how he wanted to act: "I can will what is right, but I cannot do it" (7:18). Paul was aware of the power of this hidden part of life because it kept him from doing things he willed to do and pushed him into thoughts and actions contrary to his values (7:14–25).

Why does this unrecognized anger have such destructive power? The answer is really quite simple: because we give up control over anger that we ignore. When our anger is hidden from us, we can't apply our rational capacities, our will, or our spiritual resources to evaluate and guide this anger in creative, redemptive, loving directions. Instead, the hidden anger acts in isolation, and becomes vulnerable to "the law of sin" that Paul describes (Rom. 7:25). Spending energy trying to get rid of anger usually leads to suppression, however, and is not the answer to anger's destructive potential. Yes, we often misuse and pervert it, but we must not confuse the demonic expression of anger with the capacity for anger itself. Spiritual maturity comes not in trying to exterminate anger, but in knowing ourselves well enough to distinguish between ethically appropriate, constructive anger and inappropriate destructive anger. We have significant control over what we allow to trigger our anger, and how we express it. The Creator has granted us freedom to decide both when to get angry and how to respond with our anger.

I suggest that every time you and I run from anger, or pretend it does not exist, or do not attend to it, we have collaborated with sin and made ourselves more vulnerable to the demonic: we have "let the sun go down" on our anger and made "room for the devil" (Eph. 4:26–27). The more ethical choice is to take responsibility for recognizing our anger, working to keep it in our conscious awareness. Then we can choose more intentionally how to understand it and express it in the most loving and creative ways.

YOU MAY BE WONDERING

Perhaps you are thinking, "If anger is responsible for all the bad stuff you've described and all the horrific results on humankind that we see in the media, wouldn't it be better if we could get rid of it?" Doesn't this reality argue for doing away with all anger? We wish we could wave a magic wand and be rid of the anger that lies behind much of the abuse, fighting, and violence that devastates God's creation. But this is not a possible solution.

First of all, our brains are wired with this capacity for anger, so ridding ourselves of it is physically impossible. We don't have the option, brain scientists have discovered, to get rid of our *capacity* to feel anger, or to live without threat, and, therefore, we all feel anger. We must accept that part of our "self" is a biological package that includes being "wired" with this capacity to experience anger. We don't have a choice. This neurological part of us cannot be ripped out (psychologically or surgically)!

Second we must ask: even if we *could* eradicate anger, *should* we? I think not. Why? As we saw in chapter 4 there are important reasons why the Creator built this capacity into our neuro-logical self. It is a capacity that reflects God in whose image we are made and was part of the incarnation as seen in the life of Jesus. So even if it were possible, ridding ourselves of this capacity would be to deny part of God's intentional creation.

7

Anger as a Spiritual Friend

Are you startled by the suggestion that anger can have a positive role in your life? Anger may feel so dangerous to you that you find it difficult to imagine anger as a *spiritual friend*. If you think of anger as an enemy, or have been exposed to anger that wounds and victimizes, then the idea of anger as a guide on your spiritual pilgrimage may seem ridiculous.

But remember that our capacity for anger is part of being created in the image of God, a gift that has been called "good" and blessed by God. I hope you will invite anger to be a spiritual ally, a partner in striving toward personal wholeness. Many things happen in life that can prevent us from growing and developing into what God would have us to be. We need to be aware of those forces that would keep us immature, dependent, or alienated.

Anger is our ally first and foremost because of its basic function: to warn us of threats to our self. As we have seen, anger arises from the anxiety we feel when our personhood is threatened. It is the early warning system that something is threatening. Anger is an ally when it motivates our defensive and

105

aggressive responses to these threats. It is part of our survival system provided by the Creator.

ANGER AS A GUIDE TOWARD SELF-UNDERSTANDING

Anger can also be a spiritual friend when it reveals aspects of our life that we need to work on, correct, and allow to be transformed by the gospel. It is a spiritual ally when we allow it to become a "diagnostic window." By this I mean that if we work to use our anger to understand why we are threatened, we have the opportunity to learn something about ourselves that we might not learn in any other context.

A fever gets our attention because it signals that something is wrong,[1] and we focus quickly on reducing the sick person's temperature. Fevers don't occur, however, unless there is an underlying inflammation, and to treat only the fever, without paying attention to the cause, would be foolish and irresponsible. Likewise, when we're angry we have the responsibility not only to make sure our anger does no harm, but to seek out the underlying threat. Using an experience of anger as a "diagnostic window," and learning what the threats really are, enables us to change our behavior in ways that allow us to love and be loved in new and wonderful ways. Some ways in which anger can be a spiritual ally by aiding us in self-understanding are: recovering our true self, identifying idols, and uncovering guilt and shame.

Recovering Our True Self

We can lose our best self in many ways. Unjust, unfair, or controlling relationships, for example, can cause people to lose their sense of self and their sense of worth. They have been robbed of the spiritual freedom[2] to think, feel, and act in ways that affect the world around them. They feel powerless and helpless, and often accept the "way things are." Instead of being threatened and angry by their powerlessness, they become passive and stay slaves to those who control them. But anger can help us recover our true selves, so that we become the type of person God intended and desires for us. And when that happens, anger can serve some of its most precious roles—defender of the self, protector of self-integrity, and guardian of the self's emotional boundaries.

> Daniel was twenty-seven years old, single, and in his third year of a graduate program. His major professor sent him to me because he was in danger of flunking out despite his outstanding ability. Daniel came willingly because he was "so depressed all the time" that he couldn't concentrate. He was also worried about what to do after graduation. He would have a master's degree but did not like the jobs available in his field. When I asked why he didn't pursue a job he liked, he said, "Mother would have a fit!"

It turned out that Daniel was preparing for a vocation he didn't like because it was the career his mother had planned for him since he was a child. As a dutiful son, he had been pretending interest in this profession, hoping he could learn to like it and satisfy his mother. His mother controlled his behavior in other ways, as well: for instance, he only dated women she approved of because he felt he should marry a person she would like to keep her happy, and he regularly spent his weekends with his mother. Daniel was trapped in an unhealthy, dependent relationship, trying to choose a vocation and mate based on his mother's approval. Over several sessions Daniel shared his story:

> Daniel was an only child born late in the lives of his parents, who had been told they would probably not have children. His mother told him often of his difficult birth and her feeling that Daniel was a "special gift from God." She overprotected him from the beginning and continued to treat him as a frail child. She mothered by "smothering" him. Daniel revealed that "Mom and Dad don't get along too

well," which may explain why, as he said, "I'm her whole life!" She monitored his every move, listened to his phone calls, grilled him about his activities, gave constant advice, and made most of his decisions. When he did not follow her wishes, she would become upset and judgmental of him. Daniel grew up believing that his mother's happiness was his responsibility (a heavy burden for a child). He was always "good" (meaning compliant and dependent) so that she would not be upset.

It was easy to hear in Daniel's voice the anger he felt toward his mother, but he himself tried hard to ignore it. Instead of recognizing and dealing with his anger, he sabotaged his own life by failing to reach a level of autonomy that would enable him to make his own decisions, take responsibility for himself, adopt a personal value system, and establish a personal identity that is distinguishable from his parent's.

As Daniel continued to recount stories of his mother's domination, he began to realize how his desire to be a mature adult was being seriously delayed by his passive dependency. In our culture people move from dependence to independence. When they become independent they can participate in interdependence: the enjoyment of mutual relationships with parents, peers, and partners. Daniel's anger was an appropriate signal that his development as an adult was being threatened by his mother's control. When he finally acknowledged his anger, it helped motivate him to begin, as he put it, "breaking away."

Daniel slowly began to set limits to his mother's involvement in his life. He asked her to stop calling every day, and he explained that he did not want to discuss his dating life with her. Soon he began going home less frequently. Eventually he chose to enroll in a different school and pursue the vocation about which he had always dreamed—being a pilot. His mother became angry and frustrated at losing his dependency, as will probably happen with any person from whom you begin to break away. But Daniel's anger, carefully expressed, became his spiritual friend and ally as he freed himself from being trapped in this unhealthy dependent relationship. Daniel was kind, but firm, with his mother, explaining his need for independence and his desire for interdependence, but then leaving it to her to make adjustments and to find her own life. Finally he became what he called "his own man" and at that point had the choice to move from independence and then to interdependence. Daniel was able to gain the freedom to seek, and then choose, the self that God wanted him to become.

Maybe you are wondering whether you have "lost yourself" to another person—spouse, child, boss, or good friend. Perhaps you sometimes feel like a modern-day slave. Ask yourself, Do I feel free to express my thoughts and feelings in this relationship without being rejected or punished? Do I have the freedom to make my own decisions about things important to me? Do I have a vote that counts within the marriage or family situation? Am I respected for my abilities and loyalty at work, recognized as an individual with unique feelings and needs? If the answer to any of these questions is no, then you might want to evaluate whether you can use your anger as a spiritual ally in changing the relationship from dependency into one of, first, independence, and then interdependence.

Anger as Idol Detector

Most Christians are committed to the First Commandment, "You shall have no other gods before me" (Exod. 20:3). Yet we constantly push the Living God from the center of our life and give center stage to the common "stuff" of life as if those things were gods. These "gods" include things such as food, which we eat with little regard for health; money, which we can seek with little awareness of greed; and jobs that can consume us. People such as bosses, children, televangelists, entertainers, and sports figures become gods for some folks. Even ideas such as religious doctrines and political systems become the center of life for some people. In theological language these become idols, inadequate gods. Worship of false gods is subtle, so we often fail to recognize when we have created idols. But just as a metal detector points to hidden metal, anger can help us detect and uncover our idols.

How does anger help? It is actually pretty easy: we feel the most anger when the idols at the center of our lives are threatened. Why? Because idols constantly need defending. False gods are not capable of bringing us real joy, providing peace of mind, carrying our hopes and dreams, or meeting our basic spiritual needs. Therefore, real life constantly exposes their inadequacies, and so we become threatened and angry on their behalf.

> Jackson visited his pastor, at his wife's insistence, because he had gotten angry at his two children, nine and eleven years of age, for hiding his cigarettes. The children wanted him to quit smoking and argued that it was an addiction, an argument he disputed. The pastor, whom Jackson respected, invited him to be curious about how he could get angry over something as supposedly unimportant to him as a cigarette. Jackson was willing to discuss this issue in the context of what he believed as a Christian. The metaphor of "idol" caught his attention and enabled him to admit that "perhaps he did need the cigarettes more than I have admitted." This metaphor enabled him to decide, on the basis of his faith narrative, to apologize to his children and begin a program that he hoped would help him "break the habit."

Our relationships can also be idolatrous. When we give too much credence to one person's opinion, their approval can become an idol in our lives, and we live to be pleasing not in God's eyes but in the eyes of a parent, a spouse, or a friend.

> Madeline was constantly angry when visiting her parents. She and her husband both believed that the anger stemmed from her mother's constant put-downs and criticisms. Her mother was critical of Madeline as a wife, mother, cook, and homemaker, and even of how she dressed. And indeed, much of Madeline's anger was due to her mother's comments.
>
> Things changed when Madeline began to understand her response to her mother. Madeline confessed that she had

always been desperate for her mother's approval, which she had never received. Her mother's criticism was a constant threat to the need for her approval. During the process of exploring this anger in the context of her faith, Madeline was able to realize that her desperate need for her mother's approval was a type of "worship." She decided that her mother's opinions had indeed become an idol. We explored the possibility that if she moved God into the position she had heretofore granted to her mother, then perhaps she could trust God's acceptance and love. This idea produced a significant change in Madeline's feelings for herself. She decided to trust the perceptions that her husband, sister, and best friends had of her rather than her mother's critique. Once she had taken her mother out of the idol role, she was also able to accept her mother's "critical personality," as she called it—but it was no longer central in her life.

Another common form of idolatry is the commitment to sports teams. You probably know people who get really angry when their team is ridiculed or criticized. The team has become their central commitment in life, their highest value, that which they adore, and even teasing can feel threatening.

If the idol is a spouse or someone you live with every day, the task of "de-idolizing" that person is more difficult. The way you act is already familiar and comfortable to the other person. You will have to change patterns of relating that work well only for the other: perhaps you handle all the finances, make the meals, make sure the car is maintained, watch only the TV shows that person likes, run all the errands, and put up with criticism and belittling. So if you change your behavior, this person may be upset, as Daniel's mother was. But once you are in touch with your anger, it will give you the courage to move ahead.

In each example a human attachment has gained the significance usually reserved for God. The living God needs no defense, but idols are weak and do have to be defended—hence our anger on their behalf when they are threatened. Many of us hide this idolatry from ourselves, but when a situation arises that threatens one of these "hidden" values, our angry response clearly identifies our idolatry.

What about your anger? Sometimes when you ask yourself why you felt threatened, the answer will reveal an idol. Remember that part of dealing with anger creatively is to assess the validity of the threat. It is our Christian responsibility to determine whether those things we're invested in are in sync with our faith or whether they represent our "worship" of values that don't measure up to our faith. Then, as Jackson did with his cigarettes and Madeline with her mother, we can choose to push these idols out of the center of our life. We can invite God back into the center. Worship can once again focus on the Living God, who does not need defending. Then we give thanks for anger's role as a spiritual ally.

Uncovering Guilt and Shame

You know how awful it is to realize that you have broken a pledge, hurt someone, cheated, told a lie, acted illegally, or disobeyed your conscience. The guilt and shame can feel so terrible that often we deny or suppress the feeling. It is easy to rationalize guilt by explaining it away, or denying responsibility for what happened, or blaming someone else. Anger propels us on the path toward self-discovery and spiritual growth by allowing us to uncover guilt and shame we might have been denying.

> Marilyn and Ken brought their seventeen-year-old daughter to see me at the counseling center. The daughter had recently told them she was having sexual intercourse with her boyfriend, which made them upset and angry. Their value system about premarital sex had been threatened. They were also afraid that the daughter would get pregnant. Marilyn was so furious that the first session was very difficult, filled mostly with hostile accusations and judgments from the parents, particularly Marilyn. So I cut the session short and scheduled a separate conference for the parents in

which we could pursue why Marilyn had so much hostility. Ken finally broke his silence and suggested that Marilyn tell the whole story. She resisted, but finally broke down in tears as she confessed that this daughter, who was sleeping with her boyfriend, had been conceived out of wedlock.

Marilyn had been embarrassed by her own violation of her moral code and felt ashamed that she had fallen short of her ideal. She had coped for seventeen years with this threatening experience by suppressing her memory of it and had never dealt satisfactorily with either her sense of guilt or the shame she felt at her behavior. Her anger at her daughter's behavior revealed this unresolved situation. Her daughter's behavior was threatening, but the bigger threat was Marilyn's own guilt. Facing her anger allowed her to identify her guilt and deal with it in the context of her Christian faith. Anger served as a spiritual guide by uncovering her guilt and giving opportunity for reconciliation with both God and her daughter.

So another reason to be sensitive to your anger and evaluate it carefully is that you might find that the threat represents guilt that you have ignored. When trying to understand a particular incident of anger, you can ask, "Could I be feeling guilty? Is this intense anger related to something I have done, or not done, for which I feel ashamed or embarrassed?" If the threat *is* related to guilt, then your faith can guide you through confession, repentance, acceptance of forgiveness, and restitution, which allows you to move forward into renewed spiritual vitality. And again you can be thankful for anger as a spiritual friend and guide.

ANGER AND HOPE

We are created with the capacity to project ourselves into the future through our imagination. We use this ability to dream about what lies in front of us. The specific plans become our goals, ambitions, and purposes—what I call our "future stories."[3] These "future stories" contain our expectations and anticipations, including our faith about God's involvement. They become the heart of our *hope*.

Unexpected life events, however, such as accidents, health crises, the inability to get pregnant, failing to get a promotion, or military deployment, can threaten our hopes and lead us toward feelings of hopelessness or despair. A common symptom of hopelessness is the inability to be angry at events that would normally be threatening, the same kind of passivity that Daniel exhibited in the previous section. But anger is our spiritual ally when it enables us to challenge these threats to our dreams by pushing us toward actions that sustain or renew hope by creating new "future stories." Anger becomes an advocate of hope by motivating us to defend ourselves, to fight to survive, and to resist the unfairness in our lives. Anger can be an expression of protest and resistance that leads to confrontation and change; it is therefore a sign that we are still hopeful.

As counselors, my wife and I prefer working with partners who are angry with each other rather than indifferent toward one another. When partners are angered by threats to the relationship, they are probably still invested in each other and have hope that the relationship can be rescued or transformed. Apathy, however, usually indicates that a partner has emotionally "moved out" of the relationship and doesn't care enough to feel threatened.

Brittany had lost interest in her relationship with her husband Jordan, but finally agreed to try marriage counseling with him. He was fearful that she was considering moving out, and she admitted that this solution was in the back of her mind. Why? Over several sessions she described all the things about him and the relationship that made her angry. Although she had kept some of them to herself, she had tried to express many of them to him but been thwarted by his unwillingness to admit there was any problem. Jordan admitted that he had failed to listen, but confessed that the reason was that he feared his own anger would, given Brittany's sensitivity, make things even worse. After reminding each other of their still strong love, they realized that not dealing with the anger was causing the loss of hope and made a covenant to begin dealing with angers past and present in order to restore intimacy.

Is your life filled with hope? If not, can you identify what situation or relationship seems to make you feel hopeless, powerless, sad, or depressed? Have you accepted that situation or relationship too easily? At some point you must have been threatened by this situation that is robbing you of hope and joy. What happened to your anger? Have you suppressed it? Getting back in touch with that anger can provide the courage to take the risk of changing yourself (even if that upsets somebody), to demand changes in other persons, or even to leave a situation or a relationship in order to recover the abundant life God desires for you.

ANGER PROTECTS INTIMACY

The experience of Brittany and Jordan described above also illustrates the next point. Like many Christians, they had grown up thinking that love and anger are opposites. What they discovered was that not dealing with anger had interrupted their intimacy and put their relationship at risk. They had used silence and withdrawal to keep the anger and conflict down, which kept them from the deeper levels of communication. Their sexual encounters became less frequent.

Brittany and Jordan learned that all intimate relationship contains behaviors, attitudes, conflicting values, and unmet expectations, which create threats to each partner and, therefore, generate anger.[4] When one or both partners deny or avoid their anger, it's increasingly difficult to be honest and to trust the partner; communication can become constrained; a feeling of distance can arise; and their sense of intimacy can be compromised. This anger, of course, becomes dangerous itself if it is allowed to "go bad" and become bitterness, jealousy, or resentment, which then spoils sexual attraction.

Anger has served as a wake-up call for many couples, providing the motivation for changing attitudes and actions that move the partnership in jeopardy back toward intimacy. How does this happen? The process discussed in chapter 5 identifies the importance of being willing to recognize and acknowledge the anger, rather than keeping it secret (sometimes calling for confrontation), and then figuring out what values, beliefs, expectations, or needs have been threatened. Brittany and Jordan carefully followed this process and then explored possible ways to change the threatening patterns. Then they made covenants about changes that reduced the threat to both partners, which enabled them to solve conflicts and reestablish the intimacy that feeds love.

Do you feel disconnected or even alienated from an important person in your life? Pay attention to any anger that you may feel. Do you trust the other person enough to share in appropriate ways the threats that have occurred and the anger that seems to have driven a wedge between the two of you? Maybe that person cares enough to listen, and to respond by sharing what has been difficult for him or her. The free flow of honest communication, including the anger, has the potential to break down the dividing wall of hostility. The anger can be the spiritual guide that directs you back to the intimacy that once existed in the relationship.

GETTING BACK IN TOUCH WITH GOD

Being angry with God can undermine the level of intimacy we feel with God—the relationship can become strained and our own spiritual journey delayed or completely derailed. Being open and honest with our anger can allow it to be a guide to restoring the closeness and can revitalize our trust and faith in the God who loves us.

Anger at God occurs most often when life is not going well, particularly when a crisis occurs and you ask the "Why?" questions. Why did this happen? Why now? Why me? Why my family? Accidents, death, unemployment, rejection, being deceived, and other painful occurrences make you wonder: if God is a good, caring, all-powerful, loving God, then why didn't God prevent this tragedy?

> He was a pastor in his early fifties whose young adult daughter was killed when her car was hit by a truck that careened through a stop sign. When he began expressing his anger in a letter to God, he listed all the ways in which God could have intervened: "You could have let the driver be sick and not go to work that day, delayed him at one of his stops, had him stop for coffee, go to the bathroom, or hit one more traffic light—any number of things that would have caused him not to be at that intersection at that moment. Just several seconds would have made the difference and nobody would have known. Why didn't you?"

You can feel this pastor's disappointment that the loving, all-powerful God in whom he believed didn't prevent this.

Perhaps you know from your own experience how it feels to wonder, how could God let this happen? If God is in control, and God's will is always being done, as you may have learned, then you may wonder: Why didn't God direct those bullets in a different way? Why didn't God block that clot before it reached his heart? Why didn't God keep Hurricane Katrina at sea? Why didn't God answer my prayers and help me quit smoking?

Or perhaps you feel that "God did this to me," and wonder, What did I do to deserve this?

> One young woman who had a miscarriage told her pastor that she felt that God had done it to her—causing the miscarriage as punishment. Though she did not know why she was being punished, killing her unborn child was, she felt, out of proportion to whatever sin she had committed. If she needed to be punished, that was acceptable, but she was very angry that God chose to take her punishment out on an unborn child. It was harsh and unfair and directed at the wrong person.

Perhaps you prayed with faith, expecting God to respond, but your prayers for protection were not answered; God did not intervene.

> A father who had just heard from the chaplain that his son had been killed in a military action stood up from the kitchen table, turned around, and smashed the wall with his fist, looking up to heaven and shouting, "God damn you God!" And then his first words to the chaplain were, "I've been praying every day for my son, and where was God, that SOB!"

God had failed to protect his son, and this man was clearly angry that God's promise of hearing prayer and offering protection had been broken.

If you learned that feeling angry with God is disrespectful of God's authority, or a sign of rebellion, or reveals a lack of faith in God's will, then you will have trouble sharing or even admitting your anger with God. Some people even fear that God will punish them for daring to be angry. They forget that "Perfect love casts out fear."

If this is your experience, you may move quickly to squash any anger you feel with God, but your anger will not disappear. As with unrecognized or unexpressed anger in any relationship, it hides in the back pockets of your mind and heart and can become a stumbling block to your spiritual growth.

It could be a clue that you are angry at God when you experience a lack of freedom and spontaneity in your faith: worship becomes dry, impersonal, routine, or meaningless. Maybe you have been angry with God, but have chosen to ignore it? If so, it would free your spiritual self if you could trust God enough to be straightforward with that anger.[5] Leona provides an example. After describing the intense anger at God she felt because of her son's disability, she wrote

> It was not until I got to the lowest point in my life that I was able to go to God and be totally honest about my feelings—the despair, the sadness, and the anger. I finally got to the

point that I could scream, yell, and cry. It was only when I got to this point that I felt a peace I had not known for three years. Once I was able to be honest with God, I experienced the grace and peace that only God can provide.

If anger at God is keeping you from enjoying a close relationship with God, let anger be your spiritual friend and ally. Why not try to express the intensity of your grief and anger about the problems that threatened your trust in God? Express your disappointment and outrage; tell God that you feel unloved, given over to evil, picked on, punished undeservedly, left unprotected, and abandoned. I can promise you that the God of our Lord Jesus Christ will listen.

Ask yourself about the angers that led you to pick up this book. Let your anger serve as a diagnostic window. What do you need to learn about your anger in order to discern the threat? Return to chapter 5 and review the steps involved in dealing creatively with anger. To understand our anger and take appropriate steps to resolve it is a door into abundant life.

A Final Word

Our capacity for anger is a gift from the Creator that, though it has the potential for harm, serves useful purposes in human life. Destructive experiences with anger can make us yearn for a magic wand that would rid us, and the world, of this anger. Anger, however, cannot be banished from our lives, but should be accepted as a potential spiritual ally, learned from, and used in the service of love.

We must accept that anger is a universal human experience, a God-given emotional response in the face of threats to our physical, social, psychological, and spiritual well-being. To pretend that anger is not part of our human experience is foolish and from a faith standpoint distorts God's creation.

Understanding anger from the biblical and theological perspective I have described makes a new ethical stance imperative. It is our ethical responsibility to handle anger in ways that are life-enhancing, for both ourselves and our community. Scripture reminds us that we have the freedom, indeed the responsibility, to handle anger creatively. After questioning Cain about being angry (Gen. 4:6–7), God reminded him that he could "master" sin that was lurking at the door. The author of Ephesians also believed that we can choose to keep anger from being destructive, advising readers to "Be angry, but do not sin" (4:26) and then instructing them that as followers of Christ they should "put away" bitterness, wrath, slander, and malice, those expressions of anger that are destructive rather than redemptive. Both these Scriptures and the social sciences support the idea that we have control over how to express our anger. We can express our anger effectively and redemptively if we exercise our freedom to handle it wisely and lovingly.

All parents and grandparents are concerned about the constant exposure of children and adolescents to real violence, such as drive-by shootings, being beaten up at school, verbal and physical abuse at sporting events, but also violence in the media: movies, TV shows, rap music, videos, and video games. Violence is often the expression of anger that is not handled creatively. We must teach our children and grandchildren to be creative with anger, rather than destructive. Understanding anger and how to manage this volatile emotion, therefore, seems imperative.

As Christians we are called to "the ministry of reconciliation" (2 Cor. 5:18). As "ambassadors for Christ" (v. 20) we are to speak and act so that our lives proclaim the good news that Jesus the Christ "is our peace" and "has broken down the dividing wall, that is, the hostility between us" (Eph. 2:14). We are to experience in ourselves and represent to others the unifying power of God's love. This is our "message of reconciliation" (2 Cor. 5:19). Understanding and handling our anger creatively is important to our witness.

Notes

Chapter 1: Reconsidering Anger

1. See Andrew D. Lester and Judith L. Lester, *It Takes Two: The Joy of Intimate Marriage* (Louisville, KY: Westminster John Knox Press, 1998), chap. 4.

2. It also gave us new ways of functioning as therapists. Judy is also a Licensed Marriage and Family Therapist and a member of the American Association of Pastoral Counselors.

3. Herbert E. Hohenstein, "Oh Blessed Rage," *Currents in Theology and Mission* 10, no. 3 (June 1983): 162, sums up what some people learn in their faith tradition: "Almost from infancy one is taught to believe that angry thoughts [and] feelings are incompatible with the presence of the Spirit in one's heart." Theologian Abraham Heschel summarized this pervasive teaching within the Judeo-Christian tradition: "Few passions have been denounced so vehemently by teachers of morality as the passion of anger. It is pictured as a sinister, malignant passion, an evil force, which must under all circumstances be suppressed." Abraham J. Heschel, *The Prophets*, vol. 2 (New York: Harper & Row), 1962.

4. From sermons and devotional books, from parents and grassroots word of mouth, many of us learned that anger does not contribute to the kingdom of God ("for your anger does not produce God's righteousness" [James 1:20]) and is equal to murder ("But I say to you that if you are angry with a brother or sister, you will be liable to judgment [Matt. 5:22]). These passages, and others, are presented as proof that Christians should avoid anger.

Chapter 2: Why Do We Get Angry?

1. Questions about anger have intrigued psychologists and other social scientists for a long time, but the most exciting new information comes from neurologists. Their research on the brain is crucial to our exploration of two basic questions: Where does anger come from? and

Why do people get angry? For a more complete description of the brain and emotions, plus a bibliography of scientific resources for understanding the brain and emotions, see my *The Angry Christian: Theology for Care and Counseling* (Louisville, KY: Westminster John Knox Press, 2003). For more information that is quite readable, see Babette Rothchild, *The Body Remembers: The Psychophysiology of Trauma and Trauma Treatment* (New York: W. W. Norton & Co., 2000), and Joseph LeDoux, *The Emotional Brain: The Mysterious Underpinnings of Emotional Life* (New York: Simon & Schuster, 1996).

2. Neurological research on the brain is crucial to understanding anger. New knowledge of human emotions is an unexpected benefit of the brain research conducted in the campaign to understand Alzheimer's, Parkinson's, and other diseases of the neurological system. Using new noninvasive technology, such as brain imaging, researchers can observe how the brain functions while a person is actually feeling an emotion, including anger and fear.

3. There is a close connection between anger and fear—they often go hand in hand. Many of the same parts of the brain, and similar neurological processes, are involved with both anger and fear. They are often present in the same circumstances because both of these strong emotions are significant contributors to the "drive to survive" package with which we are created. When the brain interprets something in our life situation as threatening or dangerous it often sends out signals that we should be fearful as well as angry—part of our survival instinct. Something that frightens us may also make us angry, and something that makes us angry can be frightening. While waiting for an ambulance for your spouse who has collapsed, you might feel both fearful that your spouse's life is in danger and at the same time angry that the ambulance is taking so long to arrive. Being downsized out of a job can spark fear of financial ruin at the same time that it generates anger at those who seemingly made an unfair decision. When you are feeling either fear or anger, a further assessment will probably reveal the presence of the other feeling. For example, if our body is endangered, we automatically feel threatened and feel both fear and anger because our physical well-being—therefore our very life!—is in jeopardy. We even call such situations and illnesses "life-threatening." Anger and fear in the face of such circumstances is quite understandable.

4. For more information on the significance of future stories on how we hope, see my *Hope in Pastoral Care and Counseling* (Louisville, KY: Westminster John Knox Press, 1995).

5. For a more thorough discussion of anger within marriage, see Andrew D. Lester and Judith L. Lester, *It Takes Two: The Joy of Intimate Marriage* (Westminster John Knox Press, 1998), chap. 4.

6. Carroll Saussy presents this concept in her helpful book *The Gift of Anger: A Call to Faithful Action* (Louisville, KY: Westminster John Knox Press), 1995.

Chapter 3: What Does the Bible Say?

1. For a selective history of perspectives on anger in the Christian tradition see chap. 7 of my *The Angry Christian: A Theology for Care and Counseling* (Louisville, KY: Westminster John Knox Press, 2003).

2. See Ps. 4:4.

Chapter 4: Does Jesus Get Angry?

1. See Marcus J. Borg, *Meeting Jesus Again for the First Time* (San Francisco: HarperCollins Publishers, 1994).

2. *The Interpreter's Bible* (Nashville: Abingdon Press, 1952) vol. 8, 497–98.

3. For a more detailed account, and further bibliography, see my *The Angry Christian: A Theology for Care and Counseling* (Louisville, KY: Westminster John Knox Press, 2003), chaps. 2, 7, 9.

4. Borg and other scholars prefer this translation over "Be merciful, just as your Father is merciful" (NRSV).

5. C. S. Lewis, *Letters to Malcolm* (New York: Harcourt Brace Jovanich, 1963), 97.

6. Borg, *Meeting Jesus Again*, 46.

7. From the Gates of Chai Lectureship, Texas Christian University, Sept. 21, 2000.

Chapter 5: Dealing with Anger Creatively

1. For guidance in communication skills, including "shared meanings," see Sherod Miller, Daniel Wackman, Elam Nunnally, and Phyllis A. Miller's *Connecting: With Self and Others* (Littleton, CO: Interpersonal Communication Programs), 1992.

2. For material on making covenants, see Andrew D. Lester and Judith Lester, *It Takes Two: The Joy of Intimate Marriage* (Louisville, KY: Westminster John Knox Press, 1998), chap. 8.

Chapter 7: Anger as a Spiritual Friend

1. Willard Gaylin uses this analogy in *The Rage Within: Anger in Modern Life* (New York: Simon & Schuster, 1984), 93. Also see James D. Whitehead and Evelyn Eaton Whitehead, *Shadows of the Heart: A Spirituality of the Negative Emotions* (New York: Crossroad, 1994), 21–22.

2. See Galatians, particularly chap. 5.

3. For a discussion of "future stories," see my *Hope in Pastoral Care and Counseling* (Louisville, KY: Westminster John Knox Press, 1995), chap. 2.

4. See Andrew D. Lester and Judith Lester, *It Takes Two: The Joy of Intimate Marriage* (Louisville, KY: Westminster John Knox Press, 1998), chap. 4.

5. Henri Nouwen said, "The anger and hatred which separate us from God can become the doorway to greater intimacy with [God]. . . . It is clear that only by expressing our anger and hatred directly to God will we come to know the fullness of both [God's] love and freedom."